VOICES IN THE NIGHT

WOMEN SPEAKING ABOUT INCEST

EDITED BY TONI A.H. McNARON AND YARROW MORGAN

Published in the United States by Cleis Press, P.O. Box 8933, Pittsburgh, Pa. 15221 and P.O. Box 14684, San Francisco, CA 94114.

10 9 8 7 6 5 4

Cover design: Deborah del Castillo
Typesetting, keylining, design: Jennifer Klein

ISBN: 0-939416-02-6
Library of Congress Catalogue Card Number: 82-071369

Printed in the United States.

Grateful acknowledgement is made to the following editors and publishers for permission to reprint previously published materials:

Sinister Wisdom ("Remember", "Night Lover" SW #9, Spring 1979; "Fever" SW #12, Winter 1980; "When You Grow Up An Abused Child", "Five After Incest" SW # 15, Fall 1980), Common Lives/Lesbian Lives ("Untitled Incest Piece" CL/LL #2, Winter 1981); K.S. Brindle and Associates ("childhood" in She, 1977); Contemporary Literature Press ("childhood" in Cornucopea, 1977). "Chain" is reprinted from The Black Unicorn, poems by Audre Lorde, with the permission of the author and the publisher, W.W. Norton & Co., Inc. Copyright 1978 by Audre Lorde. "In Silence Secrets Turn To Lies/Secrets Shared Become Sacred Truth" was part of an art exhibit, "Bedtime Stories: Women Speak Out Against Incest," at the Woman's Building, Los Angeles.

This book is available on tape from the Womyn's Braille Press, P.O. Box 8475, Minneapolis MN 55408.

TABLE OF CONTENTS

Women we wish to thank include: Lyn Miller, our typist; A Woman's Coffeehouse Collective, for letting us give a benefit reading to raise funds to pay our typist; Astrid Bergie, Shirley Garner, Leslie LeFevre, Kate Moos, and Susan Norris (Cygnet) who helped us with the critical responses. Special thanks go to all the women who sent us their work or letters of support.

I, Yarrow, wish to thank Connie Wolfe for the years of incest therapy work that helped me get here. I, Toni, wish to thank Barb Meyers, Cathy Flynn, and Christopher Street for my time in their incest treatment program.

INTRODUCTION

Though incest may occur in every third woman's life, there has been virtually no attention paid to it in writing until the last two or three years. Even now, books are few and tend to be either "studies of" or one woman's story. Rather than add to this literature, we have collected pieces written by a number of women. These have the immediacy and potency of direct expression together with the form and distance that come from writing a poem or letter or short story or journal entry.

The idea for this collection actually emerged quite organically. We belong to a lesbian writers' group that meets weekly. We realized that not only were we writing poems about the incest in our childhood, but so was one other member, and a fourth said that she would be eventually. That was half our group. We speculated that other women in Minneapolis and across the country must be in a similar phase of their dealing with incest. We were soon composing a letter of introduction to newspapers, bookstores and journals, asking women to send us their creative efforts to resolve their incest experiences. The responses, both entries and letters of support, confirmed our expectation. The following collection is the result. We see this book as one of many such anthologies. Every woman who can share her experience with this ugly reality surely gives increased permission to others still frozen in their terrorized silence.

This book is about breaking silence. It is true that there are many kinds of silence, some of them eloquent, but the most eloquent silence of all can be shut out by the closed ear. That has been the history of most incest survivors—eyes averted, voices unheard. The silence of women who have been incest victims is often self-imposed. We feel shame at having been abused by those we know are supposed to love us, and the horror of that abuse and shame turns inward as the victim tries to learn what she has done wrong, why this is happening to her. The internalizing of shame and the belief that she is responsible somehow for what is done to her keep the victim silent, often for years after she is an adult and it is safe to speak. Holding this pain inside, keeping even the fact of pain secret starts a spiral that often leads to suicide—many incest victims do not survice.

The women who have written in this collection, then, are voices from those who have survived incest. Voices, women speaking, the oral telling of truths, have also been treated as a kind of silence in our culture, where "Truth" is perceived as what is outwardly defined, commonly known, and publicly acknowledged, witnessed, heard. So we the powerless, women who have been sexually and emotionally abused in the family, that place which our cultural traditions tell us is safest, most sacred, begin in this collection to redefine the parameters of our world. The world that we as women live in is often very different from the world depicted in most literature, but most literature has been written by men about women.

The practice of incest is very old in our culture and has been labeled a taboo. Those behaviors are made taboo, rather than simply against the law, which are accessible to the largest numbers within a society. Given our patriarchal system, it stands to cruel reason that fathers and other adult males would act on any feelings of power they might have toward their daughters, no matter how defenseless their victims might be. As females, those daughters do not enjoy human status; consequently, they do not deserve the same consideration as sons. Those same fathers then silence their victims by such overt means as threatening severe punishments and by covert means such as appeals to family loyalty.

Both of us are survivors of incest. For me, Yarrow, my years of personal work dealing with the impact incest has had on my life have caused me to think at length about the place and politics of incest within our society. The effects on me have sometimes seemed so far-reaching as to be beyond my grasp. Some of them have been:

—It alienated me from my parents at an age when they defined the possibilities of the world outside.

—It put me in a stance of "other" in relation to my family and the outside world.

—It alienated me from both my body and the feelings I had in it.

—It made me believe that either I was "evil" (because this happened to me) or the world was "evil" (because my parents defined the parameters of that world) or both. These became unconscious assumptions on which I acted for years.

—It taught me to hate being a woman, to believe that being a woman was synonymous with being an object to be used and abused. This alienated me from myself and other women.

—It left me with huge stores of anger which all too often were randomly vented on the world around me.

For me, Toni, the process of naming myself an incest victim has been very gradual. My issues are with my mother, contrary to most of the women in this collection and to almost all available literature on the subject of incest. For years, I acknowledged that my mother had been possessive and that her way of loving me had felt suffocating at times. For years, I also knew that I avoided relating to women my own age, choosing one lover much older and a number of lovers much younger than I. Finally, I remembered enough dreams and did enough therapy to begin to understand the sexual aspect of my relationship with my mother. For me, she was my first lesbian lover: if I doubt this, I need only to look at the Valentine's and Mother's Day cards I wrote her. The language is excessive and based on a romantic world view. As a result of my incestuous bond with her, I have often felt crazy living my life as a lesbian. While preferring women as my sexual and emotional partners, I found them terrifying precisely in proportion to their closeness to me. Obviously I never let myself get close; consequently I felt extremely deprived and lonely, since I did not choose to be close with men either. I believe this painful paradox gave me an excuse to drink longer than I might otherwise have done, since I could pretend to some kind of sexual excitement if I drank. Two years ago I went through an incest treatment program. That month of intensive work and a year of after-care sessions have given me time and the tools to understand the complex web of love and hate that formed around me and my mother, and which eventually covered any potentially-caring woman.

These last two statements are personal, while the effects of the incest experience may vary from woman to woman. But many of them are observed so often as to become common threads. They all look like and are destructive behaviors, though at the time of their initial use, they were the only means of survival open to the victim. What begins as a way to endure the madness being inflicted upon the victim becomes at some point a force over which she no longer has any control. The behaviors most often "chosen" are alcoholism, and/or drug abuse, prostitution and/or sexual promiscuity within relationships unaccompanied by cash payments. The repetitive choosing of abusive relationships whether to friends and lovers, husbands or lesbian partners. Though the current discussion of incest acknowledges the heavy incidence of chemical dependency among incest victims, little is said about the effect on sexual practices in later life. The irony of this speaks to the extreme pain surrounding the topic for all concerned. Victims need to be shown that they were trained for abusive relationships by their fathers, brothers, uncles, grandfathers, more distant relatives. Only by looking at the original sexual violation and its repercussions can the woman ever hope to change her definitions of what and who feels good around her body.

When we put these psychological effects together with the knowledge from current studies that approximately one out of every three girl children experiences sexual abuse in her family, and with figures that approximately 97% of all victims of sexual abuse are girls and not boys, we begin to place incest within the context of a sexist culture. Anything that happens to one out of every three girls is neither random nor exceptional. Instead of looking at incest as an aberration from the norm, we need to question its place and purpose within that norm. We believe that there is not a taboo against incest; merely against speaking about it. And the reason for that taboo, once examined, is clear: if we begin to speak of incest, we may realize its place as a training ground for female children to regard themselves as inferior objects to be used by men, as training that females cannot trust other females (our mothers usually didn't stop the behaviors and often passively acquiesced). Incest is an early and very effective behavioral training in powerlessness and subservience. By beginning to speak about it, we begin to threaten its continued, unacknowledged presence.

An experience I, Yarrow, had which confirms this and demonstrates the fear within the male establishment of speaking about incest happened a few years ago in a therapy-training workshop. An accepted male expert on early ego-development in children had been flown in from New York for the weekend. After he had talked at length about various early childhood traumas (sexual abuse not mentioned except in regard to seductive behavior of mothers toward young boys), he opened the floor to questions. I asked him about incest: what effects he thought it had; what had been written clinically about it. The question was greeted eagerly by both male and female therapists present. I mentioned my difficulty in finding material dealing with this topic. They agreed that incest issues seemed to come up with roughly one out of every three women clients coming to them for any reason. They too had difficulty finding therapeutic techniques and theories about incest. The expert stared at the wall for a moment, said he didn't know of anything specifically about incest, and added "If a little boy tries to talk to his mother and every time she answers him she never looks at him, that's the same thing. It's all abuse."

The implication of his remark was that all kinds of abuse are the same and therefore we do not have to look at the statistics that tell us 97% of all victims of sexual abuse are young girls abused by adult males. The obvious difference in the question asked (about female incest victims) and the answer given (about the theoretical young boy) is that we do not have statistics proving the incestual abuse of 1/3 of all young boys. Even the fact that the expert reversed the sexes of the adult and child in his answer reveals the extent to which this man was terrified of examining the relationship between psychological trauma and cultural patterns. Clearly his stance is not isolated: the dearth of writing about the effects of incest on women's emotional development is further evidence of men's unwillingness to examine a situation from which they gain.

Incest victims are often extremely young. Children are naturally eager to please their parents, to gain their love and approval. The severity of this violation of age and emotional closeness cannot be overstated. It is at the core of every entry in this collection—shock and disbelief that so primal a person is inflicting so devastating a series of blows. It is what still devastates us about our own experience.

The consciousness-raising groups of the sixties had at least one lasting effect: the sharing of undiscussable, taboo information left millions of women no longer believing that we were the only ones not to fit society's ideals. Millions of women began to view our own lives and the lives of other women as more accurate than literature, social proscriptions, statistics. We began to say aloud what our lives were, to write, to publish. Certainly this book grows out of that collective reality. We are a group of women writing out of our own experiences because we have begun to perceive that those experiences, painful as they may be, are not "private" and isolated, but a part of a whole. We, the editors, believe that the voices in this collection, all intensely personal, become a whole by being personal and true to experience itself. The experiences vary, and the patterns emerge. Many women's voices speak; each is a part of the telling.

We conceived of this collection out of our own sense of the empowering force of writing out of our worst feelings and fantasies. Bringing them out of the shadows began to get them to a manageable size. If a poem or scene could be shaped from the garbage heap of our memories, our bodies and psyches could begin to heal themselves. If letters could be written and actually sent to the victimizers and family members who supported them, we could begin to give some of the hatred and anger back to the appropriate sources and stop shouldering all the shame or blocking the reality entirely from our consciousness. From the entries we received, we feel our premise has been validated.

The pieces we have chosen here are innovative both stylistically and in terms of content. We have chosen to include letters, prose poems, and ritual as well as more familiar modes. In content, this book reflects a variety of women's stances about incest experience. Incest as a part of women's lives is rarely written about, and more rarely still by those who experience it. Conspicuously missing from this collection are the mythologized romance and seduction fantasies that male literature and art have attempted to persuade us are reality. Also missing are writings talking about the abstract significance of visits by adult male relatives to girl children's bedrooms. Also missing (generally) are dominant women as abusers. Realistically, most of the adult women—mothers, relatives—written about in these pieces are more likely to be passive and possibly reluctant accomplices.

To choose to write about this subject will open us to cries of "confessionalism." Male and male-oriented critics have often attempted to devalue women's art either by saying that it is not crafted enough, i.e. does not fit established male forms; that it is innovative; or that it is not universal. "Universal" means that it is about or from a male perspective. Since much of women's literature is about defining what our experience is, it is invalidated as private and therefore not of interest. Since we as editors are passionately convinced of the necessity and excitement of rendering women's lives into art as healing, enriching and affirmative experiences, there is little or no dialogue possible with the critic who will attempt to silence us in this way.

We wanted creative pieces because we believe that art has been from the first a potent force of the women's movement. Certainly to dare to put the final taboo into art forms is radical and brave. The power of these pieces lies first in their very existence, then in their impact through form and content. Women's writing has consistently offered new subjects to the mainstream literature. These subjects have not been exactly snatched up by that mainstream. Smoke screens of "privateness" and "confessional art" have been thrown up to let critics avoid their real feelings, e.g. envy of the energy and audience support of women writers; a sense of inadequacy in talking about such writing because of a distance (biological and chosen) from the experiences usually being written of; feelings of being threatened by formal experiments and power of voice. Incest is another such subject and will surely be found distasteful to male-oriented critics or reviewers or publishers. It will be the rare man who can be "objective" about a group of poems and prosaic pieces which at some level accuse him and his fellows of being child-molesters—this time, their own child.

So we must print our voices ourselves and review those printings and write serious criticism of such literature. We must do it because otherwise this huge reality for one-third of all women will be romanticized or buried or trivialized or mocked, like so much else of our history and culture. This story needs to be told and we believe our edition contributes to that telling, simply and powerfully, by women experienced as writers and by women for whom this is an initial breakthrough onto paper.

The act of writing is always an act of granting permission. As writers, we see on paper feelings, dreams, terrors, forms that may have haunted us for years and been kept silenced by our sense of decorum, or, in the case of incest, survival.

So we literally permit ourselves to claim the strangest, darkest, most maddening parts of ourselves. As readers, we see that others have written about their secrets and lived through it. So it becomes a little more possible for us to let our own fantasies and suppressed monsters out. Writing shapes, focuses, limits, and establishes minimal distance. Our monsters become manageable, our dreams more real if not more possible. To tell orally is the first step and in the incest program I, Toni, went through, the power of saying my story, of showing my child as I saw her for the first time in my life, unedited or censored for some parent or authority, cannot be overstated. Similarly, to witness while the other women told theirs confirmed me as "like" them not in surface details, but in basic feelings, reactions, and most of all, in the necessity for silencing our own voices.

Often we wept deeply, not from content, but from uttering the taboo words in a safe, supportive environment. To write those same stories as narrative is a second and huge step because we put form around what has seemed so chaotic, we make public to strangers the most intimate truths about ourselves. We also give up control because we cannot know how a given reader will respond to us. When we write a poem or letter or story about the impact or center of that narrative, we take a third leaping step—we dare to make art out of our female experience—to fly in the face of all expectations for what is acceptable in such forms. And again, we lose an even greater measure of control because the poem or story is concentrated and partial, leaving even more room for the reader to interpret or misinterpret. Bravery, then, seems the common characteristic of these pieces—bravery and generosity.

Yarrow Morgan
Toni A.H. McNaron

VOICES IN THE NIGHT

ET CUM SPIRITU TUO

karen marie christa minns

I want to tell you something   I want
to tell you something
that I've never told before . . .

> *"It is not the experience of today that drives us mad,*
> *it is remorse or bitterness for something which happened*
> *yesterday and the dread of what tomorrow may bring."*

I want to tell you about being seven
about growing through seven in the shadow of the Church
in the shadow of living shadows—nuns in long black dresses
whispering   litanies   sins:

> *psychotic intrusion*
> *ideological sexual contact*
> *endogamous incest*
> *misogynist incest*
> *imperious incest*
> *pedophilic incest*
> *childrape*
> *perverse incest*

I want to tell you about growing like a mushroom in the cool
  dark
of those shadows   Lolita   seductress   one-out-of-twelve
of us   if we dare tell   will remember
one-out-of-twelve
six or seven   eight or nine years old
thirty-six thousand of us every year
in the year that I was seven

one out of 25% of American women
one out of the 85% who knew the man
one out of the 58% who sat down with the man at dinner
who had knowledge of the man
and took that knowledge inside of herself
where it burned
who took that guilt inside of herself
as she'd been taught under the dark-winged gaze of the
　　Church
I want to tell you a secret that was buried
in the graveyard of my seven year old mind,
a corpse of a secret with strands of blame still clinging
to its face . . .

　　"Depression and guilt were universal clinical findings."
　　"58% under the age of ten."

At seven years old there was a man who was fifteen
who lived upstairs
who lived with me as family
and he would ask me
to come with him
to watch the small rodents he kept
caged in his room
to come with him
when they were mating and watch
he would whisper
"That's what fucking is like."
I want to tell you how heavy
a fifteen year old man's hands are
on your shoulders
when you are seven
How they have the weight of the Church
in them, the weight of silence
how they are great gray mollusks
leaving a trail of slime

as they slide below your shoulders
how they burrow into your jeans
and tear with fingers as sharp as teeth
at your clothes
how they seek the too-small room of your womb
and beat themselves against the walls until
the walls are bloody
how they are cold as any cold thing
in your seven year old nightmares, how they are death.
"This is fucking." he says
his tongue an eel in your ear, whispering, snaking
its way deep into the brain
where it will live for years
"This is fucking."

> *"A common experience in the victim is to leave the
> body—to tune out—to experience out-of-the body con-
> sciousness. Results and symptoms of incest occurrences
> include: distance, feeling different from one's peers,
> isolation, dislocation, inability to connect."*

> *"58% under the age of ten."*

I want to tell you what it like
to be dared,
to be told that if one is brave
one jumps from ten-foot high trees,
one plays with water moccasins and other dangerous snakes,
one cuts oneself with knives,
with glass, with razor blades,
one puts rodents down one's clothes,
plays 'chicken' on the tracks of an oncoming train,
lies down in the middle of the road in the dark,
To be brave means to take prick and balls in one's hands,
and tug and tug
until the moans and semen come,

to take prick and balls into one's seven year old mouth
and suck and choke
until the burning taste of sperm shoots out
into the throat and waters the eyes, the nose
Because those dares come from a man
because God is a man and the Church is God
one takes those dares
and believes—if only I can get through this
it will stop.
God will make it stop.
Like the martyrs, the Holy penitents
one just wasn't pure enough or good enough or strong
  enough
and these are tests
at the hands of a man who gets his power from small caged
  animals
and children,
at the hands of a man
whom everyone knows
and loves or seems to love,
at the hands of a man who threatens death
you are only
receiving punishment
for seven years of sins,
it is written: Witch Bitch Seven Year Old Whore
Mea Culpa
Mea Culpa
Mea Maxima Culpa . . .   in the dark corners of the house
under the black-hooded gaze of the Church
"Don't ever tell or I'll kill you. Don't ever tell or . . ."

coerced victims
passive victims
participant victims

35% are relatives

*"The youngest known victim, an infant girl of only a
few months . . ."*

The only official word for sex in the Church: adultery
in the Ten Commandments
in our Holy Catechism
in the mouths of the nuns
I was Lolita
Adulterer, Lillith in my seven year old mind.
All small things
are under the hands of God
the hands of men
the hands . . .

"Unable to connect, distant . . ."

They called me loner, sad-sack, troubled
and brooding child
hiding in the woods, the attic,
clinging to things which did not move
always fearing
the sound of beating wings, angels or demons
at my back
horrible faces pressed against the glass—
my seven year old body its own nightmare.

I will tell you a secret—
for every child under the age of ten
there are Curses
for every one of the thirty-six thousand of us every year
there are Spells
for every one of the 25% of We American Women
for every one of the 85% of us who has known her molester
for every one of the 58% of us who has lived with her
  molester
or sat down to dinner with him or driven in his car or
  watched
his t.v.

for the 70% of adolescent drug addicts who were sexually
   abused
while in their families
for the 75% of adolescent prostitutes who survived
incestuous relationships
for the 92% of female survivors of childhood sexual
   molestation
there are Spells and Chants and Curses.

We are the women who can call down God.
   We are the women who can call down God and sever those
   hands
for God is, as they tell us, a man
and men can be stopped.
We stop
by stopping the killing, the blame, the guilt
with ourselves
By burying our prayers in the Earth, for she is Mother
By burying our supplications in the ground for they are
too heavy
to be borne on the air.
We are the women who can call down God,
defeat the God they have set up as oppressor
for God is
only a man.

We are the women reclaiming the Earth.
We have left our bodies in times of survival.
We have journeyed the abyss and flown through
the Halls of Heaven
We have been scorched by Hell flames and swallowed the fire
We are the witches, the bitches, survivors and whores
We are the women reclaiming the Earth.
Our fear has turned to anger and our anger into the armor
that will protect.
We must stop the killing with ourselves,
with new voices, we must say what we see.

We are the women reclaiming ourselves, healing and binding
and protecting ourselves.

> *psychotic intrusion*
> *ideological sexual contact*
> *endogamous incest*
> *misogynist incest*
> *imperious incest*
> *pedophilic incest*
> *childrape*
> *perverse incest*

35%, 58%, 90%, 92%...

We are the women reclaiming the children
we used to be
and we will never be shamed
again.

CROSS MY HEART

Susan Marie Norris
(Cygnet)

Now from the mouth you stuffed
those nights
when I was two, three, four, five

out of the mouth that held
your organ of pleasure
your organ of abuse

repeating after you
cross my heart
and hope to die if I tell
I swore
made the sign over my heart

now from my mouth I spit these words

Old father
fearsome liar
listen to me well:
my mind forgot
my body remembers
how we rehearsed night by night.
And from those lessons
I learned to hold my silence,
my secrets.

At my request we do not speak.
And every time a memory comes to say,
"You taught me how to swim and drive,"
I turn to look and what appears
is our screen porch
the dark
those years.

MAMA TOLD ME

Luisah Teish

My Mother had always told me:
    "Baby, if a man do you *something*
        no matter if he kill you
            Get some of his hair
                in yo mouth
            Die with his blood
                in yo nails
       Then the police can find him.

But my momma didn't tell me what to do
        when a man who do me *something*
          is Uncle Freddy . . . . . .
                or even
                    Daddy

HEY, HEY ANNAMAE

Christina Glendenning

When I was growing up back East all the neighborhood women and children would sit on their green or brown painted porch steps and gossip from dinner till dusk. The custom was called stoop-setting. You got to know everyone on the block and you knew about everyone on the block. You knew who beat on his wife, who had done time and whose car had been repossessed. We kids kept our ears open. It was an uneasy neighborhood and gossip was our most important source of survival.

It was the 1950's in Pittsburgh. Most of the neighborhood didn't have televisions or televisions that worked. Our entertainment was each other. And it was hot, steelmills polluting the air with oppressive grey-brown smoke. Come early evening the porches were cool, offering easy relief from the heat of cooking and washing up. We'd sit on the stoops and shout back and forth across the street, waiting for a breeze.

Mrs. Lloyd lived in the house directly across from us. Ernie, her youngest son and mean as sin, bullied the rest of us. About seven o'clock or so she'd bring her kitchen stool onto the sidewalk and sit down. Balancing her coffee cup on her knee she'd complain about her son to all the other mothers within earshot. "You mark my words, Blanche, not even the army's gonna take that one," she'd lament over a cigarette. My Aunt Millie liked to gossip with Flo Lloyd and Mrs. Bracco. If Betty Bracco wasn't sitting on her porch it was because her husband had beaten her and she was too embarrassed to socialize. My aunt would shake her head with a commiserative nod.

"That Betty is a saint putting up with that man. That's what you get with a drinker, nothing but grief." Then she'd remember Arlene's father was an alcoholic. "Sometimes, kids, sometimes it's like that with drinking men."

32

My best friend Arlene and I would sit on our old green glider and play records. Songs that made promises of love and escape. We had been friends since we met in fifth grade. Ar was the eldest of five daughters and as her mother worked the night shift she spent most of her time at our house. We watched our neighbors and exchanged knowledgeable looks. "If my husband blackened my eye, I'd break his neck."

"Sure thing, Ar, you're sooo strong. Shit. I'd put Drano in his dinner and watch his stomach burn out. That Betty Bracco is one lazy bitch and he works two jobs. Don't ever see her cleaning house. You know the youngest kid paints his fingernails! Yeah . . . pink. She's nuts that one."

By our logic, anyone who let her old man beat on her deserved it. We would never be that stupid. It was taken for granted that we kids got beat and that our mothers either would not or could not come to our aid. And somewhere, so very close to the surface, we hated them for their weakness. We were tough in those days, our barriers carefully erected. I dyed my hair black and I smoked, butt dangling from my lip when I talked. We watched the neighborhood with bemused detachment. Street-wise and soul-weary, at sixteen we knew our lives would be different. Annamae changed all that.

Annamae Schoewalter was the fattest girl in the whole school. Her roundness was emphasized because she was so short. Buddy Weiss called her a human basketball and she would laugh, her grey pixie-pleated skirt shaking rhythmically on her hips. She shuffled when she dragged her body about, dingy anklets half in, half out of her shoes. When we were younger all the kids would chant, "Hey, hey Annamae, take your toys and go away." But she would simply join in the laughter and tag along, seemingly unaware that we were laughing at her. There was no sport in teasing a person who was too stupid to cry. She was obviously delighted to be the center of attention. As we got older, we tolerated her. Her playmates were the children younger than she and with them she seemed more comfortable. Annamae was "slow" and while we considered her retarded and we teased her we also felt some sense of protection towards her. Her family was odd and gave you an uneasy feeling when you went to the house. In our own homes if company came the fighting stopped, the beer bottles were tidied up and soon coffee was brewing on the stove. But in Annamae's house nobody even tried to cover-up and there was this feeling of walking into something that threatened to overpower you. We avoided her house and because she was perfunctorily passed from one grade to the next, she remained on the periphery of our lives.

Lunchtime always meant a cigarette break. I'd wait for Ar by her locker. "Come on, already, lunch will be over 'till you get a move on," I'd prod her. On this particular day I could tell from her sour mood that something was wrong. The past week she had asked her dad for clothes money and they fought. He had pushed her down the basement stairs and locked the door. But that was last week, past history. Of course I would never ask her what the matter was; we were best friends and didn't mess with the necessary balance we presented to the world. She would have simply shrugged in reply and returned to whatever she was doing. Being cool was important; people didn't mess with you if you kept face. I told her dirty jokes to cajole her. Soon we were laughing and ready for a cigarette in the girl's room. Phyllis and Jody were already combing their hair by the back stall when we arrived.

"Phil has a date with Ernie Lloyd," teased Jody. But she had allowed a bit of concern to tighten the corners of her mouth.

"You nuts, girl?" Ar blurted out as she touched up her mascara. "He's nasty. A good dancer but he's got a mouth on him. You know he punched out Linda when she broke up with him? Even his own mother can't stand him."

I smiled at the look on Phil's face; nearly as green as the walls and twice as faded. I lit another cigarette. Faded, dirty green walls that probably were painted when my mother was a junior. More than likely she stared at that same chipped plaster. I reminded myself to ask her when I got home. It would give us something to talk about. I broke into the silence, "Hey, you heard Joyce Weiss is preggers? My aunt says. . . ."

The finger-smudged door slowly opened. The familiar shuffling came closer.

"Hey, hey, it's Annamae!" giggled Phyllis. "You want a cig, Annie?"

She shood her head and walked past us into the first stall. We ignored her as we usually did and returned to the gossip about Joyce. That was hot news. The toilet flushed and Annamae cut through our circle to get to the sink. I removed my Luckys from behind the faucet and watched her in the mirror. The amorphous features were hidden by fat.

"Come on, Annie, have a smoke. You know how? Here, watch me." Jody inhaled deeply and blew the smoke out in perfect rings. "You try," she said as she passed the butt to Annamae.

The chubby hand reached hesitantly for the cigarette. Encouraged by the friendly gesture, she tried to inhale. When she had coughed out all the smoke we laughed and took turns showing her the proper way to exhale. Jody took her eyebrow pencil and scratched an obscenity on the wall. "It matches the decor, don't you think?" she quipped at Annie.

We got back to Phil about Ernie Lloyd. What is now termed peer pressure was our way of protecting each other. Once a girl got a reputation, that was it. Not even her friends could help her and our families would force us to drop her as a friend.

"Enough, already!" protested Phil. "I'll tell him something came up. I'll pester you guys instead." We laughed. The sunlight filtered in through the dirty windowpanes making the walls appear less grey.

"Annie, you got a hickey on your neck. Look at that." Jody squealed and winked at Ar.

Annamae smiled and rubbed her stubby fingers over the mark. Her face lit up with a strange sort of recognition as she looked at herself in the mirror. Shyly, she asked, "Can I tell you guys a secret and you won't tell no one?"

"Okay, woman of the world, who's the guy?" I laughed as Ar rolled her eyes and elbowed Jody in the ribs.

Annamae beamed with pleasure. She was one of the girls at last. Her tone became conspiratorial and we formed a tighter circle. "I was sleeping last night and I woke up and guess who was in bed with me?" She began a nervous giggle in response to our stares. "My uncle."

Through the window I could see the sun dart under a cloud, the bathroom walls darkened once more. A grey-green shadow spread over Annie's face and hid her eyes from me. Jody and Phil passed a secret gaze between them. "Holy Jesus," muttered Ar.

I took the cigarette from my lip and held it under the dripping faucet. The grey ash streaked the sink. "What did you do, Annie, when . . . you saw him?" I asked nonchalantly. Cool, got to remain cool. Take it easy. . . .

"Nothing, he's my uncle silly. He likes me and buys me stuff. . . ."

Ar cut her off. "Look, Annie, what we mean is . . . uh. . . ." She couldn't finish.

Annie's eyes clouded over and the humor left her voice. "But he says I'm pretty . . . Jody . . . Phil?" She searched our faces for affirmation. I did not want to look at her. I did not want to hear her secrets. I had too many secrets of my own.

"You are pretty, sure thing, Annie . . . only . . . maybe you shouldn't tell anyone but us. A girl has to protect her reputation, huh?" My words disguised the sick feeling spreading in my stomach as my fingers traced a pattern in the wet cigarette ashes.

Annamae brightened. "Oh, I know what you mean," she laughed. "I won't tell the rest. Well, I gotta go to gym. Bye." Annie waved and smiled like she had just stopped by to tell us a really funny joke. The door closed and we heard the shuffling fade into the hallway.

Ar leaned over the sink and swore under her breath. Jody and Phil tried to giggle but could not. "Her uncle?" Ar looked directly into my eyes, looked into eyes where my father dwelt amid lies and silences. "I know she's an M.R. but. . . ." Our bravado almost failed us. "Come on, Ar, that whole family is crazy, remember?" She nodded her head, losing herself in her own private thoughts while we walked to class.

Annamae was always on my mind after the incident in the girl's room. I'd sit on the porch after dinner just as before, but it was different. The cool indifference was gone and the grey-brown smoke that hung in the air depressed me. The neighborhood houses looked older and dingier than before. I no longer smirked at the neighborhood women and their misfortunes. Pittsburgh closed in on me and escape seemed suddenly improbable. I pictured myself sitting on a different porch fifteen years later sporting a black eye every other week. The image frightened me. But it was too soon for me to realize that Betty Bracco wasn't beat because she was slovenly but that she was slovenly because she had been hit so often. Yet, the shadow of that knowledge fell across my mind and shaded my perceptions.

Annamae got pregnant over summer vacation and had to leave school. Buddy Weiss laughed for days. He said he couldn't imagine anybody making it with a human basketball. And he would dribble an imaginary ball across the floor and roll his eyes. We all told him to shove it.

I would walk out of my way to pass Annie's house trying to catch a glimpse of her, but she never seemed to be around. Someone said she had been packed off to some relative in Cleveland. Months later the family moved over to Rankin and all traces of Annamae were gone. I had asked her, manipulated, really, her soft mind into keeping silence. Her silence, my silence. But I had cunning to protect myself and intelligence to cushion my fall. She had neither and I could not help her. But I could not let her expose the nightmare of our lives because Ar and I and the rest of our friends would have gone under in its wake.

I watched the neighbors, their voices echoing up and down the street. The children playing on the sidewalk, always keeping one ear open, learning how to become victims. And I knew I had to leave, had to follow that shadow, that hint of an idea that things were really not as they seemed. I took the guilt over Annamae with me. She never took her toys and she never went away.

5 A.M.

Yarrow Morgan

The old hungry ghosts
awake
and begin to clamor
inside me,
like dogs in the kitchen
at the sound of a can-opener,
leaping up from sleep
to run back and forth,
toenails clicking
on the scarred tile floor.

I feel like a hunk of meat
salivated over.

Mommy and Daddy
rise from the dead,
their hatred
sits cold in my belly
like bad food; they crowd
the air from my lungs,
their screaming breaks me
from my dreams
to sit here shaking
in sweat-chilled skin,
owning nothing
but my tears.

DADDY'S GIRL

Gudrun Fonfa

"Right before I was born my father went overseas in the army. That was a little over fourteen years ago. I was four and a half years old when he returned. My mother and her best friend had raised me. We were very happy. Mom and Meg took in sewing, mostly slipcovers for couches and armchairs. We lived in the midwest. I've never been told the name of the town or the state, and I've never been able to remember it. It's funny what a person can't remember.

"My father realized the change in circumstances. He was outraged, and he had a gun. My mother and Meg were pretty young, around twenty-two at the time. They moved out, and took me with them to a one room apartment. My father stayed in the house, and kept everything, including the sewing machine. We were hiding.

"Then there was the divorce. My father got custody of me. Some adult, I guess a social worker, explained what had happened in the courtroom. The social worker told me what a divorce was and that my parents were parting for good. I didn't believe her. Meg and Mom were my parents and I knew they loved each other, so I didn't believe they were getting divorced. The social worker looked at me as though I were incurably thick, and explained who my parents were. She told me how lucky I was that my father had returned to give me a normal home. I was five years old.

"The first night I lived with him, he came into my bedroom. I pretended I was asleep. It was almost summer. I was sleeping in just my underpants with a sheet over me. He pulled down my underpants and said, 'You won't grow up to be like your mother, I'll see to that.' I did not open my eyes or make a sound. I thought he would leave. Instead he started to rub what felt like a mushy finger between my thighs. I started to cry. He was a stranger. I didn't know him.

40

He was my father, but 'father' was only a word. I wanted to cry for my mother to come and get me, but I knew that would probably make him angry. He tried to soothe me. He said, 'You will like this, you will learn to like this, you'll be glad I'm doing this.' Every night that week he came into my room. I hated going to sleep.

"When the weekend came, my mother came. Meg was not with her. The court said Meg couldn't see me again. I ran to the door to see my mother and he wouldn't let her in. She screamed and cried. I cried to go to her. That was the first time my father hit me. My mother came back with a policeman, who listened to my father's side of the story while my mother had to wait outside. They talked and laughed.

"I didn't see my mother again until we were back in court. My father testified that Meg was in the car that weekend visit, but she wasn't. My mother said she wasn't. Meg was not allowed to testify, and neither was I. The court believed my father. My mother was not allowed to see me weekends then either.

"I don't think I really believed I was being left alone with him. I don't think I could have stood it. My father put a box by the stove so I could cook, and a box by the sink so I could wash dishes. I thought of taking his gun and hiding it under my pillow. My stomach was always in knots.

"My father was receiving some kind of veteran's benefits. He hadn't gone back to work yet. He hated to get up in the morning and was always bringing me late to kindergarten. Sometimes he would suggest I stay home with him that day. It was sort of a game he played. One morning we were on time. I think he had an appointment in town. When I was getting out of the car, I saw my mother across the street. I was so excited, but I managed not to show it. He took me into my classroom and handed me over to the teacher. My classroom windows didn't face the street. My mother was still there when school let out. I could see her as my father drove us away. She smiled at me. She knew I'd seen her. I couldn't understand why she didn't come over. I thought she had come for me. I finally figured out that she was coming just to get a look at me.

"After that I would wake him up as early as possible, hoping to find a way to her. Sometimes this would backfire, because he would grab me and take me into his bed with him. Even though I had managed with great difficulty to dress myself for school, buttons, tights, shoe laces, everything. He would undress me. He would talk baby talk to me. He would say I was daddy's little girl, that I belonged to him, that no one would ever love me as much as he did. I wouldn't listen, I was like a robot, calculating how soon I could get us off to school. He would be lying there naked. He would show me his penis and say this is what he used to make me. Then he would put my hand on it and have me masturbate him until my hand got all messy and smelly. All the time explaining in detail how babies, and me in particular, are made out of sperm. He acted as though it were a real science lesson, and scolded me if I didn't pay attention.

"One morning after he left me at school late, my regular teacher was absent. I decided to take my chances; I snuck out. I ran across the street to where I'd seen my mother stand. She wasn't there. I looked in the bushes. I felt frantic. Finally I saw her coming down the street. She was very surprised and frightened; she wanted me to go back into school. I started crying; I told her everything. She picked me up and ran with me to the car. Once she was inside, I think she felt safer. I had stopped crying. She was looking wild eyed. She asked me questions. I told her details. She cried and cried, 'My baby, my baby, my poor baby,' gasping and choking until I became frightened. Then she tried to stop crying to comfort me. She said I never had to go back there again. It was a promise.

"Mom and Meg and I left that day in the car and drove very far. We drove all night. I got to sit in the front. When Mom drove I sat on Meg's lap, and when Meg drove I got to sit on Mom's lap. Meg's lap was better for napping because she was fatter than Mom. We sang songs and ate carrots.

We used to always sing in the car, even when we were just going to the grocery store. That night Mom sang 'Bye Bye Blackbird' about a dozen times. 'Pack up all my cares and woes, here I go . . .' I can't hear that song without crying inside. The sun was coming up when we stopped to sleep at a motel. Two patrolmen came and arrested Mom and Meg, and took me back to my father. The court didn't send my mother to jail, but they said they would if she ever entered the state I lived in again. My father said, 'Well, we've seen the last of that queer bitch.'

"I was waiting for her. I was afraid he could tell. I was absolutely expecting her to come for me. He would say, 'We sure showed her.' Sometimes the 'we' referred to him and me. That made me so angry that he should think I sided with him! I never showed my anger; I knew better. Usually the 'we' referred to him and the courts and the cops. He said the police had slapped Meg and Mom around good, because no man likes a lesbian. He made me afraid for Mom and Meg; I felt guilty for wanting them to come back and get me regardless of the risks involved.

"What seemed like a long time later, she came back. I was six. My new school had been informed to be on the look out for her, and they were. We didn't get very far at all. My mother was sent to jail.

"My father and I moved to Florida. He got a good job there. He noticed that I was having trouble making new friends. So for my birthday my father took all the kids in my class to the circus which was traveling through town. He had a gruff kindness. He had a really generous, actually an extravagant side, that made me almost love him. Loving him made me so confused that I hated him for confusing me.

"My father got married. Her name was Anita. I liked her okay and she liked me. She was very young, about seventeen. My father stopped coming into my bed for a long time. Then it started again. Only slightly differently. He seemed angrier. He would cover my mouth with his hand, so Anita couldn't hear me if I tried to scream. It was also the first time he actually put his penis inside of me. It hurt and burned worse than anything. He said new things, like he preferred my private place to Anita's because her's was hairy.

"I realized then that he was doing this to Anita too. I felt sorry for her. I thought of her more as an older sister. I was almost eight; I tried to kill myself. When I didn't die, I told Anita what my father did to me at night. She washed my mouth out with soap. She said I was a crazy liar. She said God would punish me for trying to break up her marriage. She was pregnant. She stopped liking me then. She told my father and he beat me and kicked me. All my baby teeth that were left got knocked out. He said that no one would believe me. They would say I was jealous, and that I wasn't grateful for the nice home I had. He said he would kill me if I ever told anyone again. I didn't care if he killed me. I wanted to die. But, I didn't tell. I believed him about the world. He was my father. He always won against my mother. I knew he would win against me. I would run out into the field and dig a deep hole and bury my face in it and scream.

"I still thought about Mom and Meg. It helped, but hurt in a funny way to think about happy things we had done together, like planting the garden and the time we made a scarecrow for the corn. I had a friend over to play and we were allowed to help. Meg said we'd have to make it extra scary to scare off those rowdy crows that we got coming around. And, Mom said those crows would just think we made them a snacking perch and spend their days on our scarecrow's shoulder. We used some of Daddy's clothes that were still in the closet. Mom said this was a job for an executive, so she dressed the scarecrow up in a dark blue suit and tie and hat. It was so funny. When my friend's mother came to get him for supper, she about died laughing. She said, 'Yep, the scariest men wear suits.' Sometimes when my father goes off to work in his dark blue suit, I see that old scarecrow.

"Anita had baby after baby. I helped raise three half-sisters and a brother. My father bragged about being virile.

He used condoms with me. Weekends he would send Anita to visit her mother with the kids. I was not really welcome. I would try to stay away all day at the library. I was supposed to clean house. Anita got on a kick of saying how lazy I was. I would try to get my housework done early in the morning before she left. He had always made a habit of sneaking up behind me. I would never run the vacuum unless one of the kids was in the room with me. I hated to take showers for the same reason.

"My father would make up stupid nicknames for me. There were times he would say I didn't look anything like him, that I probably wasn't even his kid, that my mother lied to him, she could have been pregnant by any number of men who were after her. I knew I was supposed to be upset by this, but I wasn't. Anita sometimes joined in, especially when the kids were in bed and I was doing my homework at the kitchen table. They would wander in to make a drink. She would say to him that all my studying and good marks proved I couldn't be his. And he would get angry, but not at her. He would say he didn't know why he took me to raise when I wasn't even his. Sometimes I thought I would go crazy listening to them. She would say he'd been tricked by the court into saving me from the perverts. He would make a sort of gallant bow in my direction and say he was too much of a gentleman to do anything less.

"The year I was thirteen he built a partition around my bed to separate it from where my younger sisters slept. I watched in dread as it went up. He said a teenager needed her privacy. Anita was teasing me about not having a boy-friend. She gave me a lot of advice: 'the most important thing for a girl is a good reputation.' She told me to be care-ful to stay a virgin or no boy would marry me. My father said I was going to have to beat the boys off with a stick. That night in my sleep he cut off my hair and my fingernails.

"Anita was actually angry with him, I thought on my behalf. They had been fighting for years now, but never over me. She yelled that now for sure I would take after my mother. My father panicked, but then smirked his usual grin and said he'd taken care of that. Then he told all the children about my mother 'the evil lesbian who went to jail.' He told them to report to him if I ever touched my sisters. They had to be mean to me to stay on his good side. As far as I can tell my father never touched any of the other children, except I noticed him acting strange around the baby. She will be four soon, and I heard him call her by my name. I actually thought of telling Anita. She doesn't love him anymore. If someone else told her maybe she'd believe it. Whenever I tried to stand up for myself or any of the kids, she'd say, 'they put girls as crazy as you in mental hospitals for less than that.'

"Then two weekends ago my father brought home two friends of his from work. He took me aside, and in his most threatening tone told me not to call him Dad. He told them I was the cleaning girl. Then he told them that I was really his girlfriend, and he started kissing me and pinching by backside and grabbing my breasts in front of them. They were all drinking beer and trying to make me drink some when Anita walked in. She was home early. I was so relieved to see her. Then she turned and yelled at me, and called me a whore. My father promised to beat it out of me.

"So I've done the only thing I could think of. I ran away. I took the grocery money, and I hitch-hiked. I don't think they can find me here in New York City. I'm going to get a job. I'll send the money back. I don't think I look fourteen. I've passed for eighteen already. I plan to save some money and then I'm going to try to find my mother and Meg. Won't they be glad to see me."

MOTHER-RITE

Toni A.H. McNaron

I slashed your cunt
and now mine bleeds
bright red spatters in my early morning bowl
no thought of menses   only murder

I raise my phantom knife
and bring it down, down into your fat flesh
I cut stomach, breasts, and thighs
to shreds, you hear me? shreds
so die, damn you, die;
no use to writhe before me
smiling through your well-kept teeth

I want to kill you all at once
not like you did me
drop by drop and lie by lie
for years you gnawed me to the bone.
I shook within so no one had to see
or tend to me.
All for you, the tending
all for me, the tremor.

I stopped your nerves completely,
shut up your words, collapsed your heart,
and with it part of me that saw you,
pillow woman stuffed with deathly love,
looming over me.
I do not see you any more,
I see an unfamiliar void   waiting.
I mean to fill it starting now,
as, resting, finished,
I close my eyes and breathe
to the bottom of my cunt, alone.

Noreen Firtel

My father
Has been to an analyst
many times.   He
knows
how to
do the right things
think the right things
and feel the right things.
And I don't.

My father
smoked pot
once.
He doesn't-need-it-he-gets-high-on-life.
And I can't.

My father
has divorced
twice.
He is hard with his women.
And I'm not.

> *My father*
> *has touched my body*
> *many times.   He*
> *knew*
> *how to do the right thing.*
> *And I didn't.*

My father
is modern
occasionally.
He is living with a woman.
And so am I.

IN SILENCE SECRETS TURN TO LIES/
SECRETS SHARED BECOME SACRED TRUTH
a performance ritual about incest

Terry Wolverton

This performance was created as part of an art exhibit called "Bedtime Stories: Women Speak Out About Incest," which opened on October 18, 1979 at the Woman's Building in Los Angeles. Curated by Paula Lumbard and Leslie Belt, this exhibit is the first cultural event to explore incest from the perspective of the incest survivor.

The installation consists of a 6' X 6' environment defined by a blood-red canopy suspended from the ceiling. Hanging from the canopy are dozens of blood-red, crepe paper streamers. These do not appear festive; rather, macabre. Handwritten onto each streamer is a "don't say"—that is, a truth that I have not been supposed to express.

In the center of the area is a 2' circle, which is bordered by 13 hanging black streamers. On these are written the lies I told myself. Inside this ring of black is a chair and a music stand, on which rests a notebook. The piece is lit from within this inner circle.

I walk into the darkened gallery. I wear white. My hands are crossed over my mouth. Light finds me as I enter the room and follows me to the performance area. Walking, I whisper behind my hands:

Self	Secret	Silence	Lies
Self	Secret	Silence	Lies
Self	Secret	Silence	Lies

49

I repeat this slowly, growing louder each time, as my hands slowly move away from my mouth. I gaze at my open hands and chant:

> In   silence   secrets   turn   to   lies.
> Secrets are sacred truths—the Self, unshared becomes
> death   silence.

My mood changes, and I begin speaking to the audience, though still half to myself. I become a child. I do not "play" a child, but I allow myself to go into my own child self, to speak from that open and vulnerable place. I cuddle a small soft toy lamb.

> I always wanted to be a good girl.
> Good girls are treated better   abused less
> I wanted to be treated better   abused less
>
> A good girl knows: certain things are expected.
> Obey the rules
> Be nice
> Don't argue
> Suffer   quietly.
> I tried to meet these conditions.
> My family, that is
> my mother and my step-father (whom she married the
>   day I turned 5),
> my family
> rewarded me, as I was often reminded,
> with: a roof   over my head
>   and food
>   and clothing
>   and what, in my family, was called love.
> If I was a good girl
> I was secure in these things.   If not
> the threat that all would be withdrawn.

So I was a good girl
but I was never innocent.
I already knew too much about the world, about violence
  and fear.
I was full inside of rage and upset—
(in my own world I was defiant, furious and independent)—
I knew I was not really a good girl
but I could   I must   pretend to be
pretend to be loving   pretend to be happy   pretend to
  belong
pretend not to know   not to be afraid   pretend not to
  be angry
pretend to be polite   pretend to obey
pretend to hear nothing   pretend to tell the truth.
The truth!
I filled up inside with all the truth
that was pretended not to be.

The mood changes, I move into a dream-like chant, but tense
and energetic:

Don't, don't say, don't say, don't say
Don't, don't, don't say, don't, don't, don't say
Don't say, don't say, don't say . . .

I move under the blood-red canopy, moving through and
behind the hanging streamers, confronting their messages,
groping wildly at them. I go deeper and deeper into them.

Don't say: No!
Don't say: I am angry!
Don't say: Please don't get drunk tonight!
Don't say: Daddy, I don't want to watch you pee.
Don't say: Stop screaming at each other!
Don't say: I wish Daddy wouldn't walk around the house
  without clothes.

Don't say: I want a lock on my bedroom door.
Don't say: Don't hit her! Stop hitting my mama!
Don't say: No!
Don't say: Mamma, why do we stay with him? Please
   leave him!
Don't say: I am angry!
Don't say: Daddy, please slow down, don't drive so fast.
Don't say: Daddy, stop touching my breasts.
Don't say: I hate you—you don't care about me!
Don't say: I want to kill myself.
Don't say: Please stop drinking. Don't drink anymore.
Don't say: Don't shoot her! Please don't shoot!
Don't say: Daddy, I won't touch your penis.
Don't say: No!
Don't say: Mama, please don't take him back!
Don't say: Mama, take my side, support me!
Don't say: I feel insane!
Don't say: I am angry!
Don't say: Daddy, I won't give you a bath.
Don't say: I can't stand this anymore! I hate the way we
   live.
Don't say: I'm leaving forever.
Don't say: Mama, I won't compromise anymore.
Don't say: No!
Don't say: I am angry!
Don't say: I'm an incest survivor.

survivor   survivor   survivor   survivor

. . . survivor. And though, I pretended to be a good girl,
I did not obey "Don't Say."
That's right, I said it all, I said everything,
I told the truth, I was not silent!
But because I was a
good girl
I wasn't heard.
Such things could not   must not   be true

in the life   of a good girl.
What happens when the truth is   not believed?
                                denied?   punished?
I learned that a good girl must learn to say only
what will be believed.
What will bring approval.   agreement.   love.
To be a good daughter: I said, "I love you."
To be a good-looker: I wore make-up.
To be a good hippie: I took acid, angel dust, barbitur-
                    ates, cocaine, marijuana, jones and
                    tequila.
To be a good liberated woman: I said, "Fuck me!"
To be a good rape victim: I said, "Please don't hurt me!"
To be a good lover: I faked orgasm.
To be a good woman: I said, "I don't know, I don't know
                        I don't care, I don't care
                        I don't know, I don't know
                        I don't care, I don't care"

until I no longer knew the truth. My truth
confused me—
what was expected?
what could be heard?
what did I say last time?
and what had really happened?
The lies I told to others seemed like necessity, like sur-
    vival—
I knew I was not really a good girl
But I wanted to be treated better   abused less.

I forget how to trust myself with the truth.
The lies I told myself were like death.
In lies I silenced   my secrets   my truth   my Self

The light inside the area fades up slowly, illuminating the
center for the first time. I confront the 13 black streamers,
moving around that circle. As I read the lie written on each

one, I respond by tearing it from the ceiling, throwing it on the ground.

I tried to make myself believe.

Believe: That deep down inside I am Ugly, but on the surface I can pretend to be beautiful.

Believe: That I am not angry at anyone. That I do not know what I am feeling.

Believe: That I am not like anyone else in the world. That I am alone.

Believe: That the more lovers I have, the more invulnerable I will be to love.

Believe: That if I never ask for what I want, if I pretend that I don't want anything, I will never be disappointed.

Believe: That I am sexually frigid, incapable of experiencing pleasure or satisfaction.

Believe: That I can be free of my family, my childhood.

Believe: That I'll always be a victim, there's nothing I can do. That I can transcend being a victim.

Believe: That I am mad. That my truth is evil and crazy, can't be real.

Believe: That the world around me is mad—and I can trust nothing there.

Believe: That I need to protect others from my own truth.

Believe: That I *can* protect anyone from my truth.

Believe: the 13th Lie—that I was silent.

Believe: I was not silent!

What happens when truth is spoken and not believed?

When truth is denied?   negated?   punished?

Truth must be shared   and heard.

The Self must be shared   and heard.

I am now inside the circle. I pick up a silver bowl full of salt, and begin to spill it on the ground, casting a circle around the chair, then moving into a spiral until I am again outside the canopy, casting a circle of salt around the entire area. I call these names:

BIA   PAULA   JOANNE
ARLENE   SUSAN   JERE
NANCY   LESLIE   BETSY

These women, and many more—my lesbian family,
  my community—
have shared my Self with me
have supported me to speak the truth
and committed to hear it.
You give me courage.

I re-enter the canopy area, walk again through the red streamers, and sit in the chair in the center. I place the notebook in my lap, open it and begin to read:

Dear Mother,
On the eve of my 25th birthday, I decide to stop being
  a liar.
I confront you with the truth that I was sexually mo-
  lested by your husband when I was a child.
"Did he have . . . *intercourse* with you?" you ask.
"No" I answer, and you are relieved.
I noticed that you are not surprised by this truth, but
  rather surprised that I have spoken it.
I have broken a taboo   the words spoken   irretrievably;
I cannot take them back   and I can never again pretend
  to be your good girl.
Nothing can be the same for us now, though we may
  pretend it is.
I don't want to pretend it is.
"Why didn't you tell me before?" you demand
  suspiciously.
I am guilty. I have been a liar/why am I now telling
  the truth?

"Why do you tell me now? Just when things are going
   good for me.
Are you trying to punish me?" You look so dangerous in
   your guilt and grief that I almost wish I could restore
   the calm between us,
silence this secret I have spoken.
"No" I reply. "I do it for myself. To value my own truth.
It is for my own life that I tell you."

I have to remind myself that it is not I
who brings this pain into our lives
I have to remind myself that ending this silence is a gift
that I give to my life, and to other women's lives,
and that, ultimately,
this is the most sacred gift that I can give you,
Mother,
my truth.
With love, your daughter, Terry.

After a long pause I rise, place the notebook, opened, onto
the music stand. I move back outside the canopy area, and
face my audience.

I invite you now
to enter into this space, where secrets are spoken,
to share your secrets
by writing them in my notebook.

Secrets shared   become sacred truth.

Light on me fades out, but the inner light in center of circle
remains on, as I exit the gallery.

CHILDHOOD

Kathryn Ann Jones

childhood
at ten
your life should be
   games
   balloons
   looney tunes
till the man comes along and shows you
what growing up really means
   not just hair under your arms
impossible
people don't do that
so he showed me
   but don't tell your mother
         my wife
         our secret
   and don't let any boy do this to you
         ever
         or i'll kill him
but daughter wouldja
wouldja do it to me just one more time
just
one
more
time

TUCKED IN

Janice Maiman

Please mama, let me go to sleep tonight before they come,
  before
He comes mama, he comes, and he doesn't turn on the light,
  he
Turn it on mama, please turn it on, turn
The blanket isn't long enough, it isn't
The toes, the toes show, they show, and he
He comes mama, he comes, and he tucks me in, and
It on! mama *please* turn it on, turn
Tell him I'm sleeping, okay? tell him to go away, tell him
The blanket's okay, it's okay, it's
The lips, mama they're wet, and he licks them, and
Mama, stop clattering your coffee cups, he comes! he
The fingers pinching, and it was clay, it was
Mama, stop playing cards, he comes! he
It was clay sweating, it was like clay, it was
Just tell him I'm sleeping, just tell him
The blanket's okay, it's okay, it's
Prodding mama, and his nails, they hurt, mama they
I don't say a word, I know, I don't say a word.

It's okay mama, it's okay.
It's just the cold mama.
Just close the window.
Close the window.
I'll be okay.

BLACK GIRL LEARN THE HOLINESS
OF MOTHERHOOD
for Cynthia

Susan Chute

Black girl comb her dry wiry hair; pull it back in a ponytail jus by her right ear. Black girl look inta her chocklut face, steal a dab of her mamma's rouge, rub it deep on her cheek. Black girl makin her lean face full & ready.

Black girl jus leven years old look in a mirror all cloudy. She thinkin, "Yu ugly, child. When yu gonna be old nuf to smile like yo mamma?" She studyin some rusty lake in the iris of her left eye. Then mamma call, "Willa, whassa matta wid yu? Can't you hear Lana whinin? You gonna tend her?"

Black girl say nothin, jus walk to the bedroom fulla purpose, grab up Lana who wuz screamin from the floor & throw her on daddy's bed, shakin the child's legs even harder than they already kickin. She get a disposable diaper & undo Lana, noticin her shit the same color as that rusty lake & the chocklut face she wuz fussin over seconds ago. Lana yellin harder so Willa pin the diaper real tight & wonder who decided diapers should be white. Mamma shoutin, "Willa, why she cryin so bad? Whatchu doin?"

"Shhhh," say Willa to Lana, "There gonna be things hurt worse than you hurt right now." Willa dust white powder all over the baby's legs. She say, "This make you smell good," and tease a smile from Lana, busy tryin to grab Willa's hair pinned tight.

Black girl mashin potatoes & stirrin gravy for the Sunday meal, wink & giggle wid Daddy, while she think, "I do more than mamma here." Black child Willa wonder, "Do he know it's mamma's rouge?" Waitin while he rub her mamma's belly full with nother child, Willa worry, "Maybe he just be pleased wid me cos mamma pregnant & she no good for mucha anythin now." Mamma sayin to her, "Honey, they boys is fightin. You think they finished dressin?" So Willa go to see if her brothers is ready to go.

Willa sit back of the church wid foldin chairs stead of
pews. She holdin Lana & mamma holdin Dorie & both of
them wondrin who gonna hold the new baby at evenin
services. Lotta flowers at this service cos this is a funeral for
the white lady used to help wid the singin times past. Willa
rub her fingers on her dress, tryin to rub off the touch of the
white lady's wax skin feelin jus like the leaves of the flowers.
Willa never saw as many flowers cept at the flower show last
summer. Bet her mamma wouldn't get that many when she
die. Willa thinkin of the pure cold skin of the white mamma
& the delicate petals of the lilies & then she thinkin of Lana's
live warm shit like her own hot brown face which she cover
now wid rouge.

Daddy up there at the pulpit talkin now, bout the good
person the white woman wuz, now gone to bliss in heaven &
streets & castles made a solid gold. Willa recall when she ask
about that, her daddy open his mouth & show her his golden
teeth, sayin it wuz god's personal gift to him, and god spoke
to him through the gold in his mouth, and that wuz how he
preach. She member how many times she touch those teeth
wid her tongue an it feelin smooth & cold & bitter. She fraid
god gonna talk wid her tongue coverin the gold sometime,
an daddy not gonna know what god is sayin to him.

Her daddy up there still preachin but Willa not lissnin
now. She watchin a spaghetti sauce stain on daddy's suit,
thinkin, "It the same color as the first nite when he touch
me & the blood trickle & he call it the RED SEA OF MOSES
& say god be very pleased cos we wuz lovin people."

Willa look where the dead lady lyin. The dead lady a
good mamma, her daddy sayin. So many flowers, all white &
orange & purple & red coverin & climbin the walls. The smell
make Willa almost faint, like when her daddy fill her deep
inside, makin her body jerk & shake, & then her daddy
whisper, "god is here" oh so gentle, marvelin & winkin.

Now her daddy sit down & her mamma give the baby to
him & get up to sing clear & slow as dreamin. Black girl
thinkin, "Mamma beautiful, more pretty than me even when

she pregnant." Willa look at her mamma's teeth shinin white & brighter than daddy's gold as her mamma sing, "Steal away, steal away, steal away to Jesus."

Black girl know now. She understandin bout death. She know the dead white mamma goin far away to the heavenly kingdom where she run her tongue in the mouth of the Lord, fulla bitter golden laughter. Then that mamma be filled wid Jesus till she ache & shake. Cos Jesus probly need lovin like all daddy.

Anna Kore

1.

I run tiptoe, barefoot
across the cold porch floor
each morning
to throw yesterday's skirt
into the pile of armpit smells
of underpant smells

the basket is large enough
to hold a sleeping child
it's on top of the green tin rinse tubs
I can't see inside

I would jump to help
my dirty skirt
reach its proper destination
but my hand might bump a gun

Pa's six or eight rifles and shot guns
hang over the clothesbasket
waiting actualization

> *Don't touch the guns*
> *They could kill you*

Boom. It would go off, I know
A gun shouldn't go off by itself
Pa's gun would

2.

I wash dishes
saved up all day
seven eaters, three meals each
Mother puts them away
It's after supper and it's winter
Pa has time
He's done the chores early
Now he sits at the other end
of the table
reads jokes aloud
from this month's
Reader's Digest
He laughs so hearty
we laugh too
even Mother

3.

I've wanted a B-B gun a long time, think I'm old enough, but
my sister doesn't want any dumb gun so I suppose I'll never
get one or grow up to be like my Aunt, Pa's sister, who goes
hunting with him and is his equal in almost every way, no
one else does Pa let be his equal, a gun, just a B-B gun, boys
my age have 22's, I know, maybe only boys can handle that
much power, that much danger, or get to my pocket knife
is questionable enough, no sense to push my luck, stride
home from school, up the quarter-mile of gravel, the
propped-up barn, the sheet white house looking sunny
because it is my birthday, 13 years old, 5 left to go

> *Until you are 18, you are responsible*
> *to your mother, even after that*
> *if you're not good*
> *any place else would be worse, they'd*
> *put you in a reform*
> *school like a prison, you*
> *won't get away that easy*

"Your father is out doing chores, go out and find him, he
wants to talk to you," I'll be safe, I am the birthday princess,
I believe in fairies and I never put caterpillars in jars, at least
not since I've been able to read so I know they need to be
free, I go, I find Pa feeding the pigs, the spears of blue grass,
the dry board fence between us

> *Don't play near the pigpen, those sows can*
> *get wild and break down*
> *the fence take this garbage*
> *to the pigs now do as I say*

Pa in denim of gradated shades, rumpled coat to gun barrel
legs, I stand back, I don't want to see Pa's boots or the mud
and manure he stands in, years later I smell pigs in the

springtime, even in town, even inside office buildings, he
smiles as he sees me, his tight smile, I do not, I wait, he sets
down the pail, steps closer, near a post, pulls a long box from
a hiding-place, my gift, he'd kept my gift with him, to be
sure he'd be the one to hand it to me, never before or since
does he give me a gift, it's a gun, a cold blue B-B gun with a
polished wood stock, he says a word to me too, hard to
hear, maybe he says "Here," maybe the smile, the word,
maybe the gun, maybe he likes me

4.

I move from table to cupboard
his eyes are always on me
gazing, half-focused eyes
always on me
I carefully leave the room
his eyes follow
when he sees I've begun to iron
he stands up
the six feet presence
walks close, sits on a chair behind me
hairy wool pants, red with black plaid
and watches
I shake silently, burn my hand
scorch a collar
he doesn't notice
Arms tight to my sides
shoulders hunched
head down
mind denying, denying
back and rump rigid
disappearing
I turn the shirt over
tug it, tug it
around pointed end of the board
I reach in short motion
for sprinkler bottle
dampen dry spots, place bottle slowly
back on table, moving
in   almost   imperceptible   steps
He doesn't notice
Out of the farthest corner of eye
I see his eyes still fixed on me
I work way around shirt end of board
neither facing him, back to him
nor side clearly visible

I concentrate fiercely on work
Either I am not   here   or   he is not   here
He notices
"What's the matter with you? You sick?
You think I was watching you?"

5.

Fighting all day.   Ma and Pa.
Blizzard yesterday.   Now it's Sunday and they're
fighting all day
again
all through the house
They don't go upstairs, seldom do. It's too cold
and because of Ma's legs
Her veins hurt, so she only goes up
when she's too mad to notice
I'll try to study up there
I wish they'd stop
the crashing, the yelling
so hard to study
What might happen:
gouges on my neck, fists
into my breasts
how long can I stand this
there's months left to winter
their voices are as clear up here
at least I'm out of the way
    Now where did she go? She's always running off
    She can't get away with that
they'll be mad if they can't find me
try not to think of them so they won't think of me
like this, anything might set them on me
If I have to go to school without my work done
with headaches again
    So you didn't make the A-honor roll Why not?
    You know you can You just didn't try
    You're a lazy, dirty, idiotic dumbbell
    Lazy — dirty — dumbbell
    Lazy — dirty — dumbbell
    Lazy — dirty — dumbbell
    Good   for   nothing
God, just to get out of here
God isn't going to help   I know that now

God does nothing   Neighbors do nothing   Church women
do nothing
they hear, they see, but they do nothing

An old man half a mile away hears in summer
comes to see what's wrong
he comes many times   he doesn't want to believe
I dream he watches through the dining room windows at
  night
I don't know whose side he's on
I dream he shoots me   Maybe to help
I still feel the wound, the hole when I wake up

    And you wife! And you, husband! And you said!
    No, you said! Well that makes me just about!
    Well, I ought to! Well, let me tell you a thing or two!
    You just love it when you make me this way, don't you?
    How dare you say that!
    What did you say? Come back here!
Heavy legs run, doors slam, muffled crying
They're in their bedroom
I sneak downstairs, out the front door

A cyclone at my back, I'm off down the lane
turn onto the long empty road toward town   Can I do
  9 miles?
Maybe a neighbor halfway will help   Maybe I'll hide in the
  woods
The woods, the woods on the corner
a mile and a half away
My dog is beside me   I hadn't noticed
We can keep warm together
Another quarter mile in an instant
We're moving

Dog has stopped
Dog is turning back

What is it, dog?   Come on, come on
I see now   The car coming   Pa in it
Run across the field   He can't drive across a field
in knee deep snow

I can't run it either, I'm finding out
Not fast enough
He's parked the car even with me
is walking across the field toward me
His long legs
His unbreakable determination

>   *You wait until your father hears about this*
>   *You know what he'll do*
>   *I'm going to call him in from the fields right now*
He's coming, I'm done   He's coming, I'm done
Too late, too slow, too slow
"Get in the car"

He parks between the empty lilac bush and still boxelder
"Why did you do that?"
"I don't know."
"There must be some reason. You can tell me."
Silence
"Is it because of your mother?"
"I guess"
"Because she keeps hashing things over and over?"
>   *What's going on here, wife? Who broke that clock?*
>   *You should've heard what that girl said to me*
>   *Mother did, Pa   She threw it at me*
>   *Settle down, wife, settle down*
"I guess. She does repeat things, like, bring up old things."
"I'll have to talk to her. Don't worry."

6.

get off me!   get off me!
I scream but he doesn't hear
words can't come out
with my head bouncing off the floor this way

He's doing it   Pa's doing it
I'm flat on my back on the cold kitchen floor
He's astride me   he rides me   his hands gripping my head
wham - wham - wham - the floor - the floor - the floor
I feel no pain
no numb either, just hum   hum   hum
above the hum   above the blurr   I see the arms
I see the shoulders   that can throw 50 pound bales
100 pound sacks all day, any day
"And you wearing too many clothes again
What's the matter with you, wearing too many clothes?
And you talking about your mother like that"
His tractor slick work pants against my bare legs
His steel cable legs clamp me in place
wham - wham - wham - the floor - the floor - the floor

Why won't he let me just pull down my skirt
Mother is watching
what is she thinking
My vagina's so cold
I might pee in my pants
I know I'll never be the same again

It was only a T-shirt
My summer camp Big Trout T-shirt
I'd worn under my blouse
so he wouldn't keep saying
my headlights were growing

SHIRLEY

Naomi Falcone

A couple of months ago I was told that you are going to marry my brother Paul in June. I'm writing to you because I was sexually abused by Paul and I think it is important for you to know. It is his responsibility to tell you though I am aware that neither he nor anyone else in the family would take that responsibility. I think you should know partly because women ought to tell each other about men who have raped them; also because if you have any daughters you may end up having to protect them from him and I'm telling you because it's important to me that I not protect Paul any longer.

When I use the word rape I use it to mean any sexual violation of me. I do not use it in the traditional sense which is defined solely as penetration. I have no memory of Paul penetrating me which means either that it didn't happen or I've blocked it out.

For about four years (between when I was eleven and fifteen), Paul used a lot of different forms of coercion on me to try to force me to have sex with him. He tried to use guilt; saying that he would die soon and did I want him to have to go find a prostitute; that I was his favorite sister and didn't I care enough about him to have sex with him. As those methods failed he became angry and said his aggression was my fault for being seductive. Being seductive I found out meant doing things like lying down on the couch instead of sitting up while playing cards with him or because he saw me naked. He would come down in the middle of the night and wake me up and tell me I was pushing him too far and often out of fear and guilt I would follow him back up to his room. When he told me to come, sometimes he would stop on the stairs and tell me not to come any farther. When he first started his coercion he said to me that he'd realized I was

72

afraid of him and therefore he had to have sex with me (I guess based on the logic that it's not alright for a woman to refuse to have sex with a man and I better get used to it). He then proceeded to hold me down on the bed and run his hands over my body while I cried. The things I remember happening are scattered and vague, I have very little sense of time sequence or how many times some things happened. Often Paul would grab me and push his body against mine. In horror I realized about a year ago that if Paul's attempts to make me feel guilty had worked on me he could have gotten me to have sex with him and I would have had a much harder time calling it rape since I'd complied with it. There's a real lag in time in my head after what I've so far described and when the last incidents started happening. When I was 15 (I think) he started coming into the bathroom while I was taking a shower. I wouldn't know he was there until I saw his shadow on the shower curtain. The first time he tried to get in with me. Sometimes he was clothed and sometimes he was naked; he would stand there and tell me how horrible I was because I was putting him through such torture. One time when he was especially enraged he put his fist through the wall by my head.

Still quite vivid for me is the intense fear. Never knowing when he would appear again. Believing I was creating it and wanting so much to stop it but not knowing how, and because of the intense guilt I felt unable to tell anyone or even run away from him.

In the one confrontation I had with him about it he told me that I must have wanted it. It is this attitude at the age of 29 that makes me believe that Paul is no more responsible about it than he was at 15. His rationalizations will free him to act out the same abuse on other women. He once had the gall to say, in front of me, to another woman that he didn't understand how men could rape women.

I know this is hard to hear. I can feel as I write this that it would be painful to read and hard to deal with. Whatever you decide to do with it, I think you should know. If you need support or want to talk about it I'm willing to talk to you.

SO WHAT HAPPENED

Eliza Roaring Springs

So what happened?
      all those years ago.
    And does it matter?
      the gruesome facts . . . the colorful details.

I only know that
      I've *always* hated my father.
    and that hate always seemed unreasonable and
      extreme
        to my sisters and mom.
When I was little—before school age—dad had a back injury,
    so he was home all the time. My mom worked.
    We played all these psychic games—ESP—he could read
    my mind—he said we were very "connected." It scared
    me.

He used to give me baths—he'd be in the tub too,
    except with his underwear on.
I still think penises are gross.
And I still don't masturbate. (although I took the
    How to Have Orgasm class and liked it for about a
    month)

I feel like a battered woman sometimes—with emotional
    scars, but no real bruises to plead her case.

It's easy for me to be celibate—I wish it weren't so easy.

    And I hate that he can still affect me so strongly.

INCEST STORY

I've existed for twenty-six of my thirty-eight years as an alcoholic. I started drinking at seven. I bought the first of many bottles of vanilla and got drunk. Ever after that, whenever I took a first drink, I drank until I was drunk. I drank to erase memories, to numb feelings that were too painful, and to keep distance from a terrifying closeness to other Lesbians. I believe my drinking at an early age was the most positive choice I could figure out for myself. I think my only other alternatives were to permanently lose my mind or to become a seven year old suicide. Only since I've stopped drinking and sobered up have I been able to remember my past and begun to take the torturous trip back, regaining the connections between my thirty-eight year old Lesbian self and the seven year old Dyke who was in a state of almost constant emotional chaos and terror.

My earliest memory of my family life is often brought back to me now whenever I'm in a close space with little free room over my head—like in the back of a camper or in the top bunk of a cabin, close to the ceiling. A family joke was often told of how when I was little and slept in a drawer of an old bureau in a closet that if I started crying my folks would shut the drawer until I stopped crying. This has been recalled to me by a series of real life fears and through frightening dreams. It seems symbolic of how I was to grow up.

I was an unwanted girl child. My mother on two occasions yelled at my father that she'd wished she'd never had me. I believe I'd have been somewhat more valued if I'd been a boy. My folks called me by boy's names until I was in high school, my patriarchal middle name is a male's name and my mother told me they hadn't even picked out a girl's name for me before I was born. I was further disliked because I was an

75

obvious Dyke by the time I was four. Much of my mother's distress at finding herself with a child who turned out to be a female and a Lesbian was from her own suffering as an oppressed woman from a poor background who'd struggled to grab some kind of economic security and pride for herself through employment as a secretary. She married my father who, as a working class man, had a difficult time keeping steadily employed and so she became a resentful and cruel mother and the economic mainstay for our small family.

I always felt grateful to my folks for letting me live and for feeding me and not turning me out of the house and for not carrying through on their numerous threats to send me to reform school. I remember at six or seven lying in bed and hearing my mother yell "I wish I'd never had her" and saying to myself "you're on your own, this isn't good, you're going to have to look out for yourself." I began, I believe as a consequence of this self-preservation, to earn money in any way I could. I pulled dandelions for five cents a bag for the neighbors, I picked bugs off garden plants in the sweltering Nebraska sun for a quarter a jar, I made earrings with the girl I was in love with and sold them door to door in the projects across the highway from my folks' house. Around ten or eleven I started getting asked to babysit and I would take any other job instead—partly because I was a butch and shovelling snow or cutting grass appealed to me more and partly because there was a deep and disturbing fear involved. I started to have nightmares where I'd see a baby in a crib being molested sexually by an older female figure. In my silent shame I assumed I was the older female and that if I ever babysat I would sexually assault little girls in cribs. I never allowed myself to babysit for young girls in order to protect them from my disgusting self. I, of course, tied this all in with being a Dyke and patriarchal society further aided in this with its false picture of Lesbians as child molesters. This was a horrible secret that I've shouldered by myself all these years. I've had this dream again recently and I know now that there was in reality a girl baby that was sexually assaulted

in her crib by an older female figure but I was not the as-
saulter. My mother was, and I was the girl baby in the crib.
The shame and terror of what was done to me created a
response that's typical of many incest survivors; we take on
the actions that were done to us and assume we did them in
order to protect those who misused us because the reality of
what happened is simply too harsh to accept emotionally at
the time.

Neither one of my parents were either physically or
verbally affectionate or nurturing with me. My mother would
flirt with both me and my father when she wanted us to do
some favor for her and my father would begrudgingly let me
go with him sometimes to the hardware store, to buy fire-
works for the 4th of July, or take me fishing with him. I
sensed from him that he felt sorry for me that my mother
didn't pay attention to me but he didn't want me intruding
in his life either. He was an unhappy, dissatisfied, silent man.
He had a gentle streak in him and liked plants and animals.
The only sharing I ever experienced with either parent was
when I'd bring home an injured rabbit or bird and my father'd try to help me nurse them back to health. This was
also the same man who'd take a bath with me when I was
little and shove my head into his limp soapy cock and who'd
thrust his limp prick repeatedly against my genitals. He
never, all the times he did this to me, had an erection. I
remember vividly at four or so running yelling from him out
of the bathroom. From that moment I no longer thought
of my self as a female but rather as a male in every way. I
was being abused as a female and I had to think of myself as
someone who had some value in life—obviously males do
and I couldn't hold my reality together anymore. In order
to escape and survive I had to become a male. I still have
difficulty thinking of myself as a female. I equate abuse and
death with being a womon. My recurrent nightmare is of a
female baby's genitals with no head or feet or arms and the
body is dead.

Almost all of the ways I now respond to situations and
other Lesbians has similarities with a scene my folks and I

played out over and over again from the time I was about six until I was fourteen. Some of its horror comes from the inevitability of the sequence of events and the monotonous surety of its at least monthly occurrence. The drama would always begin in my folks' small and crowded kitchen. My mother, just home from work, would be sitting drinking coffee, I'd be trying to slip past her and out the back door but she'd catch me with hands I still sense with a shudder as claw-like and rough, and say she wanted to talk with me. I'd slouch into a chair opposite her at the kitchen table and fidget, keeping my eyes down so she wouldn't know what I was feeling. She'd ask me a question. "What did I want for my birthday?" "Why wasn't I going to church?" "Why wasn't I more friendly to Aunt Tillie?" I'd answer, at first truthfully, but over the years with fewer and fewer words. My answer would always bring her to tears saying "I'm an awful mother," "why are you the way you are," "what have I done wrong." I'd reassure her that she wasn't an awful mother and try to frantically reconcile my truth with her tears. She'd continue crying and my father would eventually come in the door. He always seemed to burst through the door relieving the suffocating vacuum between me and my mother in the close kitchen but exploding into it with violence and rage. He'd roar at me "what have you done to your mother?" I'd jump up, sometimes over setting the chair and enraging him further. I'd stand before him in a panic explaining word for word what had happened but he'd always lunge toward me before I could finish. Thundering "I'm going to break your spirit, what's wrong with you anyway?" he'd come after me, hitting me, kicking me, pushing me, his face red, his huge hairy arms striking me. I'd hit and kick back as best I could, dodging frantically trying to escape from him in the small cluttered space. As I'd defend myself he'd yell at me "are you a boy or a girl?", "why don't you act like a girl?" I took this to mean "why don't you act like a girl and let me beat you until you're dead?" I was afraid that in his uncontrolled fury he'd kill me. I feared for my life. I felt like a rat cornered in my own house. I'd try to run out the front door if it was open but if it was locked, as it often was, I'd have to dodge and kick my way back past my father and out the back door. Sometimes he'd grab me as I flew by and more than once I remember the taste of the salty, tough, hairy skin of his hand in my mouth as I bit my way to freedom and out the door.

I'd run then, across the highway into the fields of wheat, alfalfa, clover. I'd make a nest for myself and fall face down into it, holding onto the earth, the damp curds of soil, the strands of wheat running between the fingers of my fist, their rootedness to the ground being the only force I believed to be keeping me from flying off the earth to my death. I felt the world spinning and all the people on it trying to throw me off and I had to hold on against all odds. I had to hold on by myself for dear life. I must have cried but I don't remember myself ever crying. I'd calm down by talking to myself. Then I'd go for a long solitary walk in the scruffy woods nearby or go back across the highway and onto the block and start a baseball game or some other physical activity and play my heart out. I'd play all evening hard and rough and wild until it got too dark to see and then I'd wander reluctantly back to my folks' house, all the while hoping some neighborhood womon would call to me and magically invite me to stay with her forever. I'd go through the living room on the way to my bedroom and no one would say anything. I'd go to the bathroom and lock myself in and patch up the bruises and cuts I'd gotten from my father. No one ever mentioned that I'd been hurt and I always ended up feeling it was all my fault and that I was lucky to have only gotten hurt instead of killed.

Later, after my folks had gone to bed, I'd lay there alone and listen to my mother crying and my father yelling at her to shut up so he could get some sleep. She'd keep crying and always sooner or later come into my room and lay down in my bed with her back to me. She'd say nothing but continue crying. I'd put my arm around her and comfort her and then start to caress her arms and breasts and stomach. She'd stop crying and I couldn't tell if she was asleep or not. I don't believe she was. As I got older I remember being sexually excited and that I'd push myself against her. Later I'd turn over and want to disappear into the wall. I still can feel its rough, bumpy coldness. I wanted her to respond, I wanted to be held too. I felt like I was going to die. I wanted to die. I felt lonely beyond imagination. I'd masturbate in my despair. To feel good. In order to feel something. Anything. I'm sure she was still awake. Neither of us ever spoke a word. She never touched me in response. I wanted to make love to her. I wanted her to be affectionate. It ended finally one night when I was fourteen. I shoved a wooden wedge under the door to my bedroom. She came crying to my door. It wouldn't open. She slept on the couch. She never slept with me again. She never said a word.

The next day, to end the drama, I'd apologize to everyone and then joke and amuse them back into some communication with each other. They never apologized to me for anything. I realize now my joking and play acting were hysterical. I was acting on all my fear and terror and craziness from the night before and me and my folks were laughing at my near madness.

Not so long ago, maybe four or five months, I woke from a nightmare in the middle of the night. In the dream my mother was chasing me around the living room, she caught me and raped me. I woke up terrified and went to the bathroom and discovered I was bleeding. For split seconds I couldn't tell if the dream was real or not. For the next week I was physically tense and mentally distracted as though trying to remember something but unable to recall what it was I was trying to remember. Slowly flooding back into my consciousness came the time I was eight years old and sick for two months with the measles. No one was at my folks' house during the day so I was lonely and usually feverishly ill. I'd had the memory of the only time my mother touched me as being during this time. All I'd been able to remember was her tickling my back. It wasn't a pleasant memory. It was followed by a deep void. I'd get a sinking feeling in my gut whenever I thought of it. Coming back over me were the feelings I'd had then and vaguely at first and then in repeated detail I began to remember. She'd tickle my back and then, as in my dream, she'd rape me. My mother, night after night. I'd always thought I'd almost died from the measles, but I'd almost died from her. And just as it was when she'd come into my bed, she never said a word. She'd fuck with me, then leave silently. The silence is still the most terrifying part of my memories. It haunts me. I often feel like screaming to somehow break the silence of the assault. I still feel shame that I allowed it to happen night after night after night.

I've grown while writing my incest story. It's further pushed me to reveal my feelings to other Lesbians. This is difficult for me to do because much of my early life taught me to trust no one and least of all those who I was close to or on whom I had to depend. It has been most uncomfortable to force myself to identify with the gentleness of my feelings, like my enjoyment of cats or the wind, my love for other Lesbians and my caring for myself. This is more painful than recalling terrifying or embarrassing memories. It's difficult too for me to admit how much I desired affection or any kind of favorable attention from my mother and that I long to share loving with another Lesbian, and it seems at this point something that I'm still not trusting enough to either hope for or to communicate to anyone but my most private self.

In order to survive in my family and in the patriarchy as a young Dyke I had to literally believe I was a male, I acted and still act tough. I learned to be physically aggressive and smart and to act like I didn't care shit about what anybody thought of me, least of all what womyn I cared for thought of me. For years I've kept much of myself secret from everyone and most of all from my own consciousness. I'm learning from writing this incest story to admit the painfulness I've felt all my life about the difficulties I have with transmitting my feelings and thoughts to other Lesbians. I often have strong and passionate perceptions or thoughts but, because much of my past was too hurtful for me to admit, I suffer difficulty in connecting my beliefs with my own experiences and the very deep and real feelings that give life to my thoughts. For years I numbed my feelings until I wasn't aware of any emotional range beyond hunger and exhaustion. Now I've traveled an amazing distance and am able to recognize many emotions within myself and to recall some feelings from my past. The anguish I'm caught in currently is seeing myself trying to express to another Lesbian my loving for her and it comes out either with hostility or with all the mannerisms of a 14-year-old boy. Or I attempt to share knowledge which I perceive as having been vital to my survival as a Lesbian and I'm told I'm either not making sense or that I'm spouting rhetoric.

I'm struggling with realizing that all my life I thought I was lucky if I merely managed to stay alive and now I'm beginning to believe I deserve more than a humiliating existence. I'm learning to appreciate the ways I'm tough and to want to let some Lesbians whom I trust know that I can sometimes be sad or be unsure and be gentle too and would like to be held and taken care of as well as doing the taking care of and protecting of others. I'm slugging it out with myself and other Lesbians about how I felt for most of my life that I'm a man. I'm looking at it now with a mixture of both pride and shame. I'm beginning to think it's possible to be a working-class butch who has emotions. That to be a butch doesn't mean I want any longer to be a man. I'm getting some clarity and it feels strong and positive that if I'm aggressive or outspoken or angry it isn't the male side of me expressing itself, or if I want another Lesbian to love me sexually or if I feel like crying that isn't the female aspect of myself. Those are just further ways of encouraging the patriarchy's definitions and ownership of emotional expressions. I can be tough and cry, and I'm not lost, and neither is wrong, and neither is male or female but both are me. I'm struggling to accept myself, my doubts, my fears from the past, and my hopefulness for change—my own personal growth and a revolutionary rising of all Lesbians.

I've been able to claim my past since I've been sober. It's helping me understand why I do many of the things I used to label as hopelessly self-destructive or bad behavior in myself. I feel scarred and damaged. I also feel that I'm strong to have survived the reality and to survive now the memories and to be able to gather my strength to go on to my future. The more I talk with other Lesbians the more I realize what happened in my life is a variation on a common story of incest that many Lesbians suffer through and survive. I have found that, though the pain is seering at times, we remember only what we're capable of coping with. I believe that incest, a polite word for sexual assault of children by their parents, is a form of patriarchal dominance. It's another way that men teach womyn from our earliest years that we are their victims and are seen by them only as sexual objects to be taught abuse and fear from birth. Womyn, as mothers, all too often were victims of assault when they too were young and so now sadly pass this victimizing behavior on and visit it upon many of us, their daughters. I believe incestuous sexual assault is another of the vicious forms of initiation practiced on girl children to teach us our subservient place in the patriarchy. I know that only by talking to each other, sharing what has happened to us, trusting our dreams and memories can we open this assault to each other and bring it to an end. I want no other Lesbian girl child to suffer at the hands of her mother or father what I fought my way through. I believe that no matter how cruel and uncaring a mother may be that she too is a victim of the patriarchy just as I am. She needs and deserves my understanding. She also has my anger and distrust. For the males of the patriarchy, who gain most from this assault, sometimes done overtly or covertly by mothers to daughters in many many societies, they have nothing but my deepest hatred and fear. Not until mothers and daughters can grow into a healing of our crimes against one another and then turn toward the true enemy with united forces—once again the matriarchs and the amazons—will we be able to win back our world and care for each other and the earth as sisters and Lesbians free from male domination. I have been fortunate to have received gentle and confronting support from many Lesbians who have helped me regain my footing. It has been a rough journey, yet I would take no other path. I believe in my, in our Lesbian future.

PHOENIX

Donna J. Young

Breathe.
Just
Breathe.
Forget your left knee
Jammed against the back of the seat.
Forget your right knee
Shoved under the dashboard,
Banged with each hump against a knob.
Forget the ripping, searing pain
In the place where your thighs used to come together.
Just
Breathe.
Keep your head still,
Squashed between the armrest and the back of the seat,
So you don't strangle.
Just
Keep
Breathing.
And when he's finally through,
When he climbs off your body,
And wipes his softening bludgeon with his shirttail,
When he pulls up his jocks
And tucks his shirt in neatly,
When he cautions you not to tell on Daddy,
Breathe.
For without breath you cannot live
To Avenge yourself.

HEY, MA!

Teri Fontaine

(When you are all alone
and your mother says no,
what do you do?)

Hey, ma!
What do you do when I'm crying?
Hey, ma!
What will you do when I'm dying?

Hey, ma!
What do you do when you're lonely?
Hey, ma!
What do you do for a hug?

Hey, ma!
What did you teach your daughters?
Hey, ma!
How did you teach your daughters?

Hey, ma!
What do you do when your nerves start to crack?
Hey, ma!
What do you do when your blood is on the sidewalk?

Hey, ma!
Where's your celebration of life?
Hey, ma!
What happened to my birthday?

Hey, ma!
What do you do with a husband on one side
    and daughters on another?

Hey, ma!
How did you get that way?

Hey, ma!
What did you do when I was hungry?
Hey, ma!
Did you lock your cupboards?

Hey, ma!
What did you do when I needed air?
Hey, ma!
Did you bar the windows?

Hey, ma!
What did you do when I said I was different?
Hey, ma!
Did you throw me out?

Hey, ma!
What did you do when I was cold?
Hey, ma!
Did you lock your doors?

Hey, ma!
What did you do to my sisters?
Hey, ma!
Didn't we come from the same womb?

Hey, ma!
What did you do when big sister had a baby?
Hey, ma!
Did you take her in as one of your own?

Hey, ma!
What did you do when little sister cried for love?
Hey, ma!
Did you leave her on the streets?

Hey, ma!
What did you do when your husband beat you?
Hey, ma!
Did you beat your kids?

Hey, ma!
What did you do when your husband fucked you?
Hey, ma!
He fucked me too.

Hey, ma!
Don't you mind that your thirteen year old is no longer a
  virgin?
Hey, ma!
Did you know I was raped at eleven?

Hey, ma!
Where's your love?
Hey, ma!
He fucked you over.

Hey, ma!
He fucked you over.
Hey, ma!
He fucked you over.

Hey, ma!
What do you do when I'm crying?
Hey, ma!
What will you do when I'm dying?

PROCESS PIECE: A STORY OF TELLING MY TRUTHS: REVEALING AND TRANSFORMING MYSELF
INCEST SECRET: A STORY OF TELLING MY TRUTH: NAMING MY REALITY

Joanne Kerr

I love my mother intensely. And I respect her. And now that she is divorced from my step-father, I have moved closer to her so that we may rediscover one another.

And we had to begin with the truth. I knew that I could trust her to be strong, and anyway I just couldn't keep these secrets any longer.

So I told my mother about the incest with my step-father the same night I told her that I am a lesbian.

The sharing of these parts of myself affirmed both the pain and the joy of my life and now she can love me for who I really am.

Incest secrets are the hardest to tell, because they contain such a residue of the entanglement of lies and half-truths and psychic confusion. And because incest is a reality—fathers do rape daughters—and yet is claimed invisibly and unspoken as father-right, it is a secret that in reality everybody knows about, consciously or unconsciously. My mother knew about it, remembering a letter I wrote back then. She questioned him, believed him, never asked me. It is a secret we are ter- rified of knowing, because the pain is so great, and the choices are hard. And we are not used to bonding as women; we have learned our lessons well. And even my sister and brothers knew, but couldn't or wouldn't confront it because mother would be forced to choose between her daughter or her husband.

When I told her she believed me and wanted me to tell him that I had told her. She felt vindictive and angry and hurt and guilty. I told her that I would write him a letter.

I wrote the first letter while sitting with my mother at her kitchen table. I lost that letter, and after two more attempts, finally came up with the fourth and final one. I went through a process of feeling scared about mailing it. I fantasized that he would try to find me and retaliate in some way. I finally realized that this feeling was precisely the reason why I *had* to send the letter.

I sent this letter to the man who molested me and called it sex education. I timed it so that he would receive it the day that the show "Bedtime Stories: Women Speak Out On Incest" opened at the Woman's Building in Los Angeles, California, October 15, 1979. The letter was displayed as part of the "Letters Home" installation in the show.

Telling this secret, sharing my story with my mother and with my sisters, gives me strength. I am empowered and transformed, no longer merely an incest victim—but rather an incest survivor.

Dear ——————,

On my next birthday I will be 34 years old. Approximately twenty years ago you came into my mother's life, and unfortunately also entered mine.

For almost all of these twenty years, you and I have shared a secret—a terrible secret—and one which I am only now able to confront, and understand.

I am of course referring to the sexual experiences which happened between us when I was fifteen and sixteen. I can now name those experiences: INCEST. Have you ever heard of the incest "taboo"??!

And I really never understood before what an enormously confusing upsetting and ultimately damaging experience it was for me until now. I repressed it, ignored it, didn't know what to do with it and so I buried it deep within me and kept that secret like a stone in my heart.

But I know now that one of the most terrible things about INCEST is the way that it becomes a SECRET, A DENIAL OF THE TRUTH AND SO A DENIAL OF MY REALITY.

THE TRUTH WAS, AND IS, THAT INCEST IS A CRIME, A CRIMINAL ACT, AGAINST ME AND AGAINST WOMEN . . . IT IS A KIND OF RAPE.

I now know that I am a victim of incest.

This incest secret, hidden behind lies and denials, was also a betrayal of my mother. How many times did you lie to her? How many denials, how much deceit? How dishonourable were you—are you?

It has taken all these years for me to realize that for me to remain silent means that I too must lie to my mother. I have lied to my own mother for years. Why? To protect *you*! Pretty absurd, isn't it? Mother and I have suffered because of your cheap indulgence, petty lying, stupidity, all of which is part of the incest game which places blame, guilt and insanity on the victim—me!—instead of on the adult male aggressor—you!

I want you to understand how terrifying and horrible that experience was for me. Remember? Remember?

Do you remember how you encouraged me to be promiscuous?

Do you remember how you tried to get me to be a prostitute?

Do you remember how you bribed me with money and liquor and told me to use 7-Up as a douche?

Do you remember the stuffed animals with obscene notes attached?

Do you remember the psychological torment, the insanity?

I didn't remember. I couldn't remember, for years—until now. Now I remember.

Try to imagine the effect on a young girl that the experience of having her mother's husband, her step-father, fuck her on her mother's bed has. Can you imagine?

Can you imagine the guilt, the torment, the confusion, the pain? You taught me how to lie.

WHY?

Was it carelessness, stupidity, greed, power, lust?

Were you ever ashamed? Did you ever feel guilty? Did you ever feel anything? Did you ever care?

I got an ulcer, remember?

Did you ever notice the pain I was in? Did you notice the suicide attempts, the promiscuity, the confusion, the fear, the buried rage? Did you ever wonder, as a responsible adult, if I was okay?

I've learned that the incest experience is named a "conspiracy of silence." A "conspiracy" is an agreement to perform together an illegal, treacherous, or evil act. I deeply regret that I ever conspired with you—through my fear, and especially through my silence. I kept this secret from mother, protecting you, thinking that it was best for her, confused. I write this letter now to release this secret from concealment.

Mother knows. I told her the truth. I told her about you.

I am not writing this letter to you to be vindictive, simply to be honest, and to regain my self-respect. I do not intend to discuss it further, but I do recommend to you that you now seriously think about the way you live, and the lies you tell. I hope you think about this, and try to change, because everyday, for the rest of your life, you have to look at yourself in the mirror. What do you see?

CHAIN

Audre Lorde

News item: Two girls, fifteen and sixteen, were sent to foster homes, because they had borne children by their natural father. Later, they petitioned the New York courts to be returned to their parents, who, the girls said, loved them. And the courts did so.

Faces surround me that have no smell or color no time
only strange laughing testaments
vomiting promise like love
but look at the skeleton children
advancing against us
beneath their faces there is no sunlight
no darkness
no heart remains
no legends
to bring them back as women
into their bodies at dawn.

Look at the skeleton children
advancing against us
we will find womanhood
in their eyes
as they cry
which of you bore me
will love me
will claim my blindness as yours
and which of you marches to battle
from between my legs?

II

On the porch outside my door
girls are lying
like felled maples in the path of my feet
I cannot step past them nor over them
their slim bodies roll like smooth tree trunks
repeating themselves over and over
until my porch is covered with the bodies
of young girls.
Some have a child in their arms.
To what death shall I look for comfort?
Which mirror to break or mourn?

Two girls repeat themselves in my doorway
their eyes are not stone.
Their flesh is not wood nor steel
but I can not touch them.
Shall I warn them of night
or offer them bread
or a song?
They are sisters. Their father has known
them over and over. The twins they carry
are his. Whose death shall we mourn
in the forest
unburied?
Winter has come and the children are dying.

One begs me to hold her between my breasts
Oh write me a poem mother
here, over my flesh
get your words upon me
as he got this child upon me
our father lover
thief in the night
do not be so angry with us. We told him
your bed was wider
but he said if we did it then

we would be his
good children if we did it
then he would love us
oh make us a poem mother
that will tell us his name
in your language
is he father or lover
we will leave your word
for our children
engraved on a whip or a golden scissors
to tell them the lies
of their birth.

Another says mother
I am holding your place.
Do you know me better than I knew him
or myself?
Am I his daughter or girlfriend
am I your child or your rival
you wish to be gone from his bed?
Here is your granddaughter mother
give us your blessing before I sleep
what other secrets
do you have to tell me
how do I learn to love her
as you have loved me?

TO A SIXTEEN-YEAR-OLD

Paula Bennett

Jane, Jane

What's your name

Jane:

Plain Jane,
Crazy Jane,
Jane, Jane
That brings the rain.

You say your father
Abused you, Jane,
Put his arms around you,
Stuck his penis in you.

They stuck you in McLean's, Jane.
They said you were insane.
They said it was a shame.

And after you got out,
When you murdered the baby

(Was it his, Jane, or someone else's?
Did you care? Did you notice?)
Were you someone else's jane, Jane

When you flushed it down the toilet;
Was it loathesome? Was it vile?
Did you smile
When they convicted you of *man*slaughter
because you killed his child,

Jane?

Jane, was there any pain?
Did it make you feel insane?
What's your name
Jane,
What's your name?

CLOSET

Marti Keller

She spent her childhood in a closet,
her brown hair moused with bits of
insulation.
Scent of mothballs and tissues, drenched
in toilet water,
stuck to winter coat pockets,
the scratch of tweed jackets,
clot of Persian wool,
cold glint of rhinestone buttons.

She was a child in a closet
cloaked in rough darkness,
knees scarred from uncarpeted kneeling
in afternoon confessional,
repenting her bodily sins:
raw-boned ugliness,
flaw of freckle and moles
behind pallid thigh

She rocked narrow and whispered
father, forgive me,
I am not the beautiful princess of your dreams,
not the tawny mermaid we watched in Ensensada
sunning her perfect golden ankles
you said was your vision of
loveliness.

SISTER

Jane Barnes

Janet and I could always read each other's minds. We spent countless hours analyzing our relationships with our boyfriends and talking in detail about diets, clothes, and sex. I was working as an assistant to a group therapist and trying to decide if I should go to social work school. Janet was writing computer manuals and wondering if she'd ever be a famous writer. Janet was in love with a musician named Peter and I was having quick infatuations which never lasted longer than a few weeks. It was about the time I was seeing John; when he realized I was about to fall in love with him, he disappeared. Janet was always consoling, so I phoned her and invited her over for dinner.

It was June, in the early evening, and I was watering my plants near the open window when I heard her slow footsteps coming up the stairs. She let herself in, poured two glasses of wine, and brought them in. I was still feeding my big spider fern.

"What happened?" said Janet.

"I just don't know. John was terrific. Until just now," I said. I sprayed the plants, sending up clouds that sparkled in the fading light.

"That's what you get for picking men for their expertise in bed," said Janet. "You ought to start worrying about their minds a little."

I envied her Peter. He took her to concerts and they had serious conversations about Baroque technique. And he was a gourmet cook. She had told me she'd been the first one for Peter. She said, yes and no, when I'd asked her if he was a fast learner.

I went into the kitchen to get more wine and remembered a strong joint someone had given me as a present. I loved having long conversations when I was stoned and since Janet liked to talk, I assumed she'd be the same stoned. I'd never seen her stoned.

"Want to?" I asked her, waving the joint in the air.

"This is only my second time," said Janet. I was surprised; she liked to make a show of letting people know she'd tried everything. I sat down on a hassock and she lay back on the mattress I used then for a couch. I'd put a tie-dyed cloth over it. When the sun came in that room, it had almost a sunny look. It was the opposite of Janet's place, with its dull gold walls, formal couch, and black piano.

Janet was reading an underground newspaper. I saw she had it open to the personal ads.

"You read those, too?" I teased her. "I got off on them. Very kinky."

She grinned and lay it down on the cable spool I had for a coffee table. I lit my candle and turned on "The Yellow Submarine" and lit the joint.

"Show me how," said Janet.

"Just take a long drag. Hold it as long as you can," I told her. "You might not get too high if this is only your second time."

Janet held the joint awkwardly like a cigarette. Smoke escaped from her mouth. I took the joint to show her how to do it and then handed it back. She took several drags and then I did. It was a strong joint.

"My mouth's so dry!" Janet said. "Does this always happen?"

"Yeah, and you forget what you're . . . ummm . . . ."

"But you're already doing it!" Janet laughed at me.

"I know." We laughed together.

"Oh, I feel it," said Janet.

"What?"

"I don't know. The light. I love it," she said. I looked at the pink light in the window, and when I looked back at Janet, the smile had left her face, and her eyes were lowered.

"You know," she said, "I was just thinking of Anna. I miss her."

"Anna?"

"My sister. She lives in Texas. We were very close."

I thought of my own sister who lived around the corner. She is a psychologist, conventional but intelligent.

"I always hated Marion, but I adore her, too," I said. We both smiled at the contradiction.

"Anna's . . . she was so gentle, so patient," Janet said in a low voice.

"What's she like? Funny like you? Emotional?" I asked. Janet had rarely mentioned her.

"Yeah, well, no. She still lives out in Texas. With a dope dealer. He's nice enough, I guess."

"No kidding," I said, thinking to myself that Janet was the uptight one of the two; Anna, the hippy.

"She older?"

"No, younger," said Janet. "Don't I act like an oldest?"

"Actually, you do," I admitted. Janet's very decisive, often thinks she's right, but it doesn't bother me, I'm used to it. Because of Marion.

"Maybe that's why we get along so well," said Janet. I'm your older sister."

"Really," I said, agreeing, "but you're not as bad as Marion." I started to think of ways Marion had so often irritated me with her motherly ways, and my mind wandered and I stopped looking at Janet for a moment. Her eyes, when I looked over at her, were fixed on my face, but she was remembering something, seeing something I could not.

I started to tell her about Marion, but I was very stoned, and my description of some minor faults of hers was disconnected. I didn't really notice whether Janet was following me. When I finally wound down, there were Janet's eyes again, looking wildly at my face.

"You're stoned, aren't you?" I said to her.

"You know," said Janet, holding her bare arms with her hands, "I was terrible to her. I used to beat her. Did Marion beat you?"

"Oh, yes. Only when we were little of course. I finally got taller," I said.

"I was such a bully," said Janet, looking again at something I couldn't see.

"But everyone is," I said to excuse it for her. She looked so sorrowful, so guilty.

"No, it isn't. It isn't at all," said Janet, her voice rising. "I liked it, I liked hitting her," Janet burst into tears and covered her face with her hands. I got up and went over to her, kneeling down on the floor and putting my arms around her. She struggled against me as if she thought she didn't deserve any consolation, and she shouted "No, no!" and "I'm sorry, I'm sorry!" as if Anna could hear her apologize.

Tears stung my eyes. I saw Marion's face, eyes and cheeks puffy as they were when we'd been fighting. She'd go silent on me, even if it had been her fault. Mother often punished her automatically because she was the eldest and I would never ever let her off the hook. She'd have to sit up in her room, which she hated, being claustrophobic, while the whole family ate popcorn in front of the TV.

"Don't worry," I said. I started to tell her she'd smoked too much, but I knew I was just trying to blame it on the dope. "We don't mind," I said. "It's all right with us."

"We? Us?" she said, her voice a whisper.

"Me. And your sister," I said, searching for the exact meaning of my words. "We little sisters. Did you confuse me with her for a minute?"

"I guess I did," she said, her voice calmer. She wiped her eyes. "It's strange."

"What was strange?" I asked.

Janet covered her face.

"I saw myself when I was little," she said. "We were both—Anna and I—in our bedroom. We had a large blue and white room with twin beds. Anna's was always unmade, she would never make it, and there were clothes tangled at the end as usual. She was lying there and I was standing in front of her, telling her something, a story, I guess, trying to make her laugh. She used to say I could make her laugh about anything. It used to make me feel so good. She was lying there, laughing. On her back. She was always tall and thin, like you, and she had brown eyes like yours. When I hit her, she got this look in her eyes? They were full of tears and it made me feel so guilty. It was the worst punishment, you can't imagine. Anyway, I was leaning over her, and then I began to tickle her, to cheer her up. I loved her being helpless, and my being able to make her laugh. Make her. And then she pulled her legs up, so I grabbed her wrists, they were so skinny, and I pulled them together and pushed down on her chest and shook her and shook her and shook her." Janet's voice began to tremble.

"The worst part was that I always wanted to protect her. Be her guard or something. You know, 'I'm the biggest, no one can hurt my little sister'." Janet's voice broke. "But me, me!" she pleaded. Then she cried a little and then stopped. I didn't expect her to stop so quickly. She smiled at me as if she wasn't remembering it so strongly, all of a sudden. As if she remembered she had a surprise for me. I didn't know what to expect next.

"Sarah?" said Janet.

"Yes?" I said, feeling a little like a therapist.

"It's ludicrous, I know, but I feel for some reason, It just came over me, I . . ."

"What is it?"

"I feel like kissing you. In the middle of everything."

"You mean on the cheek?" I said. I had almost turned my chin up and walked my hands across the couch to reach her when I realized what she did want. "Oh, no, I'm not . . ."

"You're not what?" said Janet. "Oh, it's just that I want you to . . . I just want to touch you . . . I'm sorry." She spoke in a whisper again. "I'm just saying it maybe."

I had never touched a woman, not sexually. For a moment I saw John floating over me as in bed; then it was Janet's face. I thought about everyone at Cape Cod. We used to get so drunk we'd fall in a heap on the floor. One night I woke up and this woman I didn't even know was looking down at me. She was naked.

I gave to Janet's face, this woman's body. Then the candle sputtered, and I reached out my hand and let the hot wax coat the tip of my finger. Janet sat motionless, watching me play with the wax; we might have been performing a ritual.

"I'm exhausted," I said, tensing my shoulders. I attributed it to the difficulty of following Janet's sudden changes of emotion. Janet sat up and stiffened.

"I'm sorry," she said. "I ought to go, I was just kidding, I . . ."

"Well, this is really heavy stuff," I said, trying to comfort her but coming off critical.

"Now why did I remember that?" said Janet, staring off across the room. "It really happened, at least I think so. I was twelve."

"What happened?" I said. Janet didn't answer. What had she meant? Had she touched her sister like that? The way she said she wanted me? And that woman, standing above me, she was like this: tentative but single-minded, covering herself as she leaned down. She apologized, too, and then kissed me. I made her go away and the next morning someone took her to the bus stop and we never saw her again. I used to think of her after she left, in heat waves, out on the deck. It was the moon. It made me restless. I hated her so much then.

I looked at Janet. She was smiling.

"You know," she said, "I know I could take you to bed if I wanted to. I know it, but I won't."

There was a challenge in her eyes, a strong light. I wanted to shut my eyes. I didn't dare say a word.

Janet blinked her eyes. "Well, I really should leave," she said and stood up. I followed her to the door and let her open it herself. She turned as she left and smiled once.

When I heard her footsteps fade, I blew out the candle and lay down on my bed and told myself she had had no right to say that. Then I hit the pillow and told myself I'd have to stop seeing her, it would ruin our friendship. She had no right to smoke pot like that if it was just going to make her crazy. That's what I thought.

But I had nothing to fear because she only mentioned it once, when she called it "the night she got so stoned." I'd been through another half dozen men by then, including one who went either way. Then I got married and went out to the coast to grad school and we never wrote. But I got a letter from a neighbor who said she'd seen Janet with a tall, thin woman. They were holding hands. She looked very calm and happy, she wrote. I dreamed about her after that, the kind of dream that leaves you tense but not frightened. There were other women in the dream, too, and we were competing for something. I don't remember for what.

MOMMY

Yarrow Morgan

Mommy,
they call me witch
when they peer into my eyes
and see you,
the ghost who flits
with manic grin
to deeper hiding.
They call me witch
who labors still
summer spring fall and winter
to learn the rites
of exorcism,
to separate the living
from the dead.

You return in dreams
sit wrapped in blankets
dying, in a tall dark room.
My lover says
we should live alone
when you are gone,
but already I fear
the echoing of empty rooms.

I peer at your pictures;
I have your coloring
a certain stance—
but mostly I look like your father,
like your exiled sister
banished when you were sixteen.

Mother, I am so sad,
I want you here to talk to.

Last week I woke
from a recurring nightmare
of running
down peeling stairs
from an upper room
where something happened
so fearful, something happened
or was about to happen
that froze my blood,
that I could not remember.

I lay awake all night
seeing those stairs before me
until I felt you jerk my arm
to pull me down them.

But before that,
before that in the upper room—
Mommy, I remembered.
I felt your hands
around my throat again
felt them squeeze my neck
as you repeated,
     "Don't you ever say that
       about your father again."
Terror and rage
were in your face;
your face was the last thing I saw
before losing consciousness.
Mommy, you knew I spoke true;
you knew that.

II

You told me it never happened,
told me to forget.
When I woke screaming
at the pink thing
throbbing above my body,
too young to name it penis,
you crooned me back to sleep
        "It's not real."
you told me to forget.

And yet,
that same crawling horror
was there
when you scrubbed me clean,
the washcloth rubbing me
red and sore.
Your anger froze me to silence.
You labeled me dangerous,
called me whore;
like your sister,
the one long-gone
who loved the wrong man,
not her daddy.

        Mommy, I'm sad and lonely.
        I want you here.   I want
        what I will never have.

I am an aging woman
learning: if there is no exorcism
if I cannot still the demons' chatter,
at least I can move them
off   away
no penis on my body
no hands on my throat.

witch-mommy,
demon-mommy,
your spells are breaking.
I crack the frozen air:
      haltingly   I remember,
      haltingly   I speak.

FEVER

Susan Wood-Thompson

A girl of six, drenched, throws the covers off.
Her parents, old and country, pack them back
around her. Feebly in the evening she plays
cards with her aunt, waiting for the little
red marks to go.

Hearts and diamonds fade,
tonight she cannot read the cards, tonight
she learns silence, what it looks like forever
behind her head.

Crafty-eared, she hears
her mother, head in apron in the kitchen,
crying out the child who has stopped stirring in her,
whose eyes burned out, crying guilt that has no origin
no name.

The child knows.   Because the old man
used to come and touch her with that thing
inside her pants, inside her brain, to tell
her forever she's a bad girl: Good girls
don't have that happen to them.   Good girls don't
go blind.

The child knows God sees everything.

"WHEN YOU GROW UP AN ABUSED CHILD . . ."

Christina Glendenning

When you grow up an abused child your vocabulary is one of objects, of images. Words such as incest or violence no longer carry personal impact. Too often they've been used to rationalize feelings too painful and overwhelming to accept. But those feelings live, buried in objects as common as a wicker clothes hamper. The white wicker hamper in which I hid from my father, a small child covering herself with soiled bed linens. Those objects invade our peace like a strap wielded by a violent hand, leaving bright red welts on the prism of memory.

I don't suffer nightmares like some: it is the mundane encounter with a white wicker hamper that shakes me. Forcing me to relive a childhood that seems so unfair, so destructive. I'm thirty-one now, living far away from my family, but so often I am that same vulnerable little girl peering through the strands of woven wicker.

Our family lived in Pittsburgh. When my parents weren't separated my father drove truck out of state. Either way, he was a stranger to my life. My mother and I and her two maiden aunts formed an extended family. From them I received a strong sense of who I was. Those first five years of life were an idyll where my individuality was encouraged. My father moved back home about the time I was ready to start school and with him came a change of atmosphere. It was both a feeling, dark and oppressive, and a physical presence that I can only compare to a volcano. I sensed I could no longer argue the appropriateness of my bedtime plead my case during meals. I went directly to bed at eight and no longer argued about eating certain foods. There were rules that I had to obey. I was glad, initially, to be like my friends and have a father at home. But there was a price to pay. The freedoms I had taken for granted ended with the return of my father and for the first time I knew authority. I did not question my father's rights over me. All of my friends' fathers behaved like that but until then it hadn't affected my life. Where once I was thought independent, my father now called me willful. I began to resent this new oppression and the man who returned to my life not as a suppliant but as an owner.

I clearly remember the evening my father first kissed me. My mother had gone to the store and I was playing with my doll house. The kiss was unexpected, full on the lips and warm, very warm. "I love you," he said.

For a child needing parental love those words are important. I couldn't understand why they made me uneasy. That this authoritative, temperamental man loved me brought a promise of better times to come. I should have been happy but I was only confused.

Each time my mother left us alone I felt an expectation from my father that I should sit with him by the television and we would kiss. During and after those sessions he was always very kind. His heavyhanded manners relaxed and I saw glimpses of freedoms I thought I had lost. But I was still uneasy and more and more I hoped my mother would not let me alone with him. I begged to go along or pretended I was ill. Looking back, I know it was his need I feared. His love was only a thinly disguised neediness that threatened to overwhelm me. My instincts knew what my child's mind couldn't know. I was right to be afraid. It was then I discovered the clothes hamper.

It stood outside my parents' bedroom close to the front door. After crouching among the laundry I'd close the cover and wait for my mother's footsteps on the stairs. A trip to the store took about thirty minutes. I would wait and mark time by the programs on the television set. I remember a time or two when he walked past the hamper into my bedroom and called my name. My fear was palpable inside those wicker walls. I expected myself to respond but I couldn't. What would he do if he found me? What explanation could I give that wouldn't betray my distaste for being alone with him? Sometimes I left the hamper early and would go sit with him, knowing she'd be back before too long. Before he could start our "game."

The more I hid in the hamper the meaner he became. My withdrawal brought little punishments or the loss of already dwindling privileges. But the more I kissed him the more intolerable my inner world became. There are two pictures I keep locked away in my grandmother's cedar chest. The first is of me taken on the first day of kindergarten, proud and spirited. The second is my school picture at the end of first grade. The spark in my eyes had gone and a limpness had replaced it. Those pictures mean a lot because twenty-seven years later I am still rekindling the light in my eyes.

When I was ten we moved to my great-aunts' house. My parents had been having marital problems again, so I had been staying over there on weekends. Their home meant protection for me; my father and I would never be alone together. There wouldn't be time for our "game." I was growing older and knew the facts of life. My father's advances were odious and I knew consciously that his needs were inappropriate. I was angry and began to avoid him. My rejection turned his neediness into violence.

One morning I slept through my alarm. Afraid of being late for school, I quickly dressed and headed for the front door. There he stood waiting for me. In my haste I hadn't made my bed and this infuriated him. He grabbed my hair and started to hit me on the back and shoulders until I ran out the door. Any small infraction of the "rules" was enough to set him off. As I sat in class I could feel the bruises forming, turning purple beneath my clothing. A few years before I had tried to tell my mother and a school counselor what was happening. Both refused to hear me and I felt shamed for saying things that obviously should have been left secret. I never mentioned it again and I lived that way until I left for college in Minnesota when I was eighteen.

Perhaps I'm most bitter about how my father's and my relationship affected my own concept of myself as a parent.

I became pregnant when I was twenty-three and after much deliberation I decided to abort. The reasons I gave for my decision were lack of money and a lot of confusion about my affectional preference. But my innermost fear was that I was emotionally incapable of being a good parent; the fear that I would imitate the man I've tried to disown in my soul. I had to come to terms with my own anger and know that it won't overwhelm me. It is very difficult to consciously denounce what I consider negative "masculine" behavior, to deny the patriarchy only to have to confront those very same feelings in myself. Perhaps that is not all bad. But it would be much easier to say those behaviors only exist "out there."

Allowing myself to have emotional needs has been another difficult task. My personal belief is that lesbians, especially those of us raised without the benefits of community, have a difficult time with our needs, anyway. Not only because they are different from the norm but because they are so traumatic to accept let alone try to fulfill. Added to that was my inner belief that to have needs is a weakness. You will either suffocate others close to you or be suffocated in turn by their needs. I am still awkward, still learning to accept my own needs as normal. Still learning to meet those needs in ways that are healthy.

Naturally, the inevitable question arises. Did my father's behavior "make" me a lesbian? Back in the days when I thought myself abnormal I leant an ear to that tired chestnut. Now I have different thoughts. I prefer women because it is in their company that I blossom, just like when I thrived with my mother and her aunts before my father reentered our lives. By the age of five I had been permitted more of a sense of myself than most women acquire in middle life—if they're fortunate. I was a female child who had defined her own space: I knew when those perimeters were being violated.

My being a lesbian means reclaiming my boundaries, reclaiming the light in my eyes. It seems more appropriate to say that my lesbianism, my childhood strength, made my father violent. I could have played our "game." I could have pleased and supplicated my father: perhaps sexual intercourse would not have been required—only a posture of feminine passivity. But I knew I had been violated and I fought. It cost me my childhood, it cost me my child and it scarred me in places where I'm the most vulnerable—but I preserved an integrity that heals.

FIVE AFTER INCEST

Ran Hall

1. trusted, shared so many years
   so much
   betrayed
   seduced in every way
   hate disguised as love shows its hand
   on a child, free woman child.
   the friend, till the end
   holding my hand
   and screwing our daughter with the other.
   when cock couldn't shaft the mother
   he pledged his undying friendship
   and fucked a child
   (he always liked tender meat)

2. i did not deny him
   love, just my body
   was my own and my mind
   believing he understood and cared.
   oh, he cared,
   cared for his loss
   the sheath for his ego.
   and he could not accept
   the rejection.

   i can not accept his action
   my mind refuses to see
   while my guts feel
   the truth

   he is a man
   man is a cock
   and a cock will fuck

he is man is a cock
and a cock hates
he is a man and man hates me
and anything that is part of me—woman
free from his cock hates free woman
free woman child.
cock fills holes
in bodies and minds
knock 'em up or knock 'em down
fuck 'em up and fuck 'em over
every man, any woman
any age any size, any woman
just a place to stick it.
the face of hatred disguised
lies
lies
lies as love
as truth, as natural
as protection
as need, as sharing
and giving, the face of hatred
shoves its way through
the face of hatred is a cock
cock is man.

i look at my daughter
and know
that she has been touched
by that hatred
knows the meaning
of being born a woman
she knows
the beneficent father
is a cock.

i did not protect her
when my mind said "fear"

my heart said "trust"
and i taught her to trust.
my guts know fear
fear is man
my daughter's taught me
what i wouldn't learn
and i can not forget.

3.   signed over by a quit claim deed
one moment his and the next
mine.

this is mine
me, i
own a house

these are mine
two children
me, i am a single parent.

me, i, mine
i am mine
alone

dissolution of a marriage
dissolves so much
more than the preacher's words.

my past remembered
dissolves
in a solution of incest

my future as conceived
dissolves
to crystallize, beyond my eyes

4.   oh, typewriter, my friend
i have shared pain with you

and joy, every hope and disappointment
i have laid on your listening keys
and you have answered with understanding words
to ease my mind
you have stored for me
the many, too many to keep inside
you have held safe and carried my baggage
leaving me light.
but friend
though your keys are warm
under my fingers tonight
you will not take this from me
though i pound it in to you
it stays with me
and will not come out
with words or tears or time
but eats its way out
through my heart.

5.   night creeps

loudly through the open windows
seeps painfully

through my skull and enters
my frantic mind crushing my search
for peace
of mind

night when

i can think, undisturbed
i am disturbed by my thoughts
spinning and swirling
sinking and rising
covered
with bile

work and read by night
till exhaustion claims me
and chains me to sleep through the day
because

night creeps

after sleep
and waking is remembering

unable to halt the flow
think, feel think feel
and it pours from under my eyelids
cold and damp under my arms

slippery on my fingertips
i am afraid

as the night creeps

Snake

Getting fucked by daddy
    sure had no effect on me.
I mean . . . it only happened once.
I wore baby doll pajamas
He had alcohol on his breath
And he *was* a Navy officer,
And he *did* say he was sorry.
But that label slut kept
    pounding through my head,
I was only good for fucking
    just like my daddy said.

And later on . . .
Climbing in and out of beds
    to an inner double time.
The men said I did love sex
    and it didn't seem I lied,
Course they didn't see the tears
    when I turned my head aside.
Yeah, getting fucked by daddy
    sure had no effect on me.

And when I became a lesbian,
    I was terrified of sex.
I felt I wasn't worthy . . . that
    love and me can't mix.
But I'm beginning to fight back,
To struggle through the pain,
To feel the layers of guilt crack.
I'm not gonna let the past
    rob me of my sexuality,
I'm not gonna let a man make a
    life sentence out of me.

FATHER (INCEST)

Miriam

father do you want me
is that why it's so important
your wanting to control me
your anger at my tone of voice
is that why it is so easy
to hate me take it out on me

beginning to realize my father's
covert incestuous desires emotional
incest.   his voice lying when he says that
he does not find the bodies of young
women near his daughter's (my) age
sexually attractive

beginning to realize my own
did I think mother a poor mate
knowing I did not have her faults
how many times for how long
father are you a type I look for
you loved me when I slept.   I used
to love him then.   no love at all.
is it true I pick men like my father

TO MIKE

Kate Muellerleile Darkstar

You have, once again, spoiled my afternoon. I thought of the abuse I received from you. Rapist, killer, abuser, traitor, brother. How I hate it that you are also my brother. How I hate the shitty things your depraved humanhood did to me. YOU'RE JUST LIKE YOUR FATHER—con, betrayer, thief of trust, thief of person, thief of my happiness.

I will never forget you pulling a knife to my throat. I will never forgive you making me be sexual with you when I was 11. I will never forgive you for violating my body. I WILL NOT—just as adamantly as you did those horrid things to me.

Right now I hate you with every inch of my sexually abused turned chemically dependent body. I hate all men for what you did to me. You had no right.

I flashed on having a therapy session with you and what I would say to you. I'm feeling real hurt until I realize that the hurt is my anger turned outside in. I said, in my mind, that I wouldn't forget the time we lived on Park Avenue and when you tried to slice my throat and when you were threatening me. I asked you if you knew what else I wouldn't forget. You said you didn't know. Where upon I replied that I would never forget that you sexually abused me. You had said that you'd wanted to teach me how to kiss. You took me into *my* bedroom, laid me down on *my* bed and took off *my* clothes, as well as your own. I hated your sloppy, slimy kisses on my mouth—I hated your body on top of mine—I hated your hands on my yet undeveloped chest—I hated you. I hate you still—because you set the pattern for me to expect that from men in my life.

That episode was so shameful for me that the only way I knew to deal with it was to hate myself and to abuse myself.

I forgot about it, soon afterwards, I'm sure, and didn't remember it again till eleven years later, when I was ready to remember—when I had some tools to deal with it. But it never went away.

I remembered it when I was having breakfast one Sunday morning with my lover. I need to say that you ruined that day, as well as many others.

THE BATH

Hia Perl

"Get undress," Uncle says
With a rasping wheezing voice
It's time for your bath
That sure is a laugh

He always helps me to undress
He enjoys this he does confess
It's time for your bath
That sure is a laugh

Get into the tub Becky dear
Get in you'll catch your death I fear
It's time for your bath
That sure is a laugh

The bath is warm and fragrant
Its warmth such a luxury
But I have just a minute for that pleasure
Cause soon I'm called a darling treasure
Now as usual he rolls up his sleeve
Oh G-d, why can't he just leave
It's time for my bath
That sure is a laugh

Oh Mommy you've talked to the counselor, the psychologist
   too
And they told you just what you must do
But you prefer him in your bed
A good lay is what you said

Mommy, Mommy why pretend you don't believe
That he has something up his sleeve

The bath was fun when I was young
But I'm almost a young lady
Oh ma he probes at me with a discoverer's hand
Trying to unearth secrets of a private new land
When I was young and he fondled me this way
I didn't understand it wasn't just for play
Mommy, Mommy have you even noticed that I'm about to
  bloom
And I can't stand your thorn in my bathing room

It's time for my bath
That sure is a laugh

Dorothy McCracken

Saturday, January 16, 1968

I'm glad today is Saturday because I don't feel like getting up this morning. I threw up a lot last night after Dad left. Mother is watching me carefully today and I can tell she is worried, but I ate some of the breakfast she brought me and it stayed down so I guess I'm O.K.

Yesterday was strange. I wasn't going to write about it, Journal, but since I can lock your drawer, I guess it won't matter. Maybe the pen can get it all out of my head. My room had been a mess for days and I'd been promising Dad I would clean it. I thought this weekend would be soon enough, but it wasn't. When I got home from school yesterday, I found Dad had not even gone to work. He was sitting on my bed looking like he wanted to ground me for a month.

Dad said he was going to spank me. I hadn't been spanked since I was nine and that was two whole years ago. He told me to take off my slacks. I was embarrassed, but I did it in a hurry so he wouldn't get any madder. For a long time he just looked at me like he'd never seen me before. Then he told me to take off all the rest of my clothes. I felt very ashamed, but I figured that was part of the punishment so I did it. I didn't like the way he was looking at me. I wanted to run, but there was nowhere to go without clothes. I hated the idea that Dad could see my whole body without clothes so I lay on his lap before he told me to and hoped it would be over soon. I thought he would never stop spanking me. After a long time he pushed me back onto the cold unmade bed and started taking his trousers and shorts off. I began to panic, but he was on top of me before I knew what would happen. Mother had warned me about the things my body would someday make boyfriends want to do, but she had never warned me about Dad.

Dad started handling me between my legs. I had learned how to make that part of my body feel really good when I was a child, but Dad wasn't doing it right. He did not make me feel nice at all. I felt like I was going to be sick when Dad put his penis where his hand had been. I closed my eyes tight, but that didn't help because I still felt Dad between my legs and he was pushing too hard. I guess I screamed because I heard me, but my voice sounded so far away. Dad pushed back and forth for awhile and then he sort of fell on top of me and stayed. I wanted to get sick all over him, but I didn't dare. I also wanted to get out, but I didn't want to wake him so I just stayed under him and tried to cry quietly as the pain died down.

A shadow moved and turned into my mother. I don't know how much she had seen. Maybe she came when I screamed. She got Dad off me and told him to leave the house. I expected her to be nicer to me, but she really blew. After all the talks we'd had about my body, she'd expected me to have the decency to keep my clothes on. She was madder at me than she had been at Dad. I couldn't answer her, but I did manage to get to the bathroom before I threw up.

After I got sick, Mother was nicer to me. She changed my sheets while I got ready for bed. Mother thought I was crazy, but I cleaned my room before I went to sleep. . . .

Wednesday, January 1, 1969

This afternoon Mother went to visit Dad. I asked her to take me with her, but she keeps saying prison is no place for a child to visit. I can't seem to think about much except Dad lately. Christmas was awful without him. I remember last New Year's Day so clearly. Mother was visiting a friend at the hospital. Dad was propped up on their bed watching the Rose Bowl. I sat next to him and he put his arm around me so I could lie back against his shoulder. It had been a long time since he'd held me like that. I felt so warm and secure. I felt like a little girl again.

Dad woke me at half-time and said he had a surprise for me. That was when he took you down off his closet shelf and gave you to me, Journal. You were the last gift he ever gave me. I asked Dad if he could think of a way to lock you. After the game, he cleared out one of his desk drawers and gave me the key. Dad could be terrific when he wasn't drinking.

It is almost time for the Rose Bowl. Maybe if I turn it on it will seem like Dad is home again. If only it were 1968 again, I could keep my room so clean that Dad wouldn't be in prison.

Sunday, January 12, 1969

We have try-outs for the junior high play tomorrow. Miss Jackson says she would like to try the musical, "Wonderful Town," with our group. I can't try out for cheer leading until spring so this musical is the best thing going for the rest of the winter. I hope I get a good part. Wish me luck.

Thursday, January 16, 1969

The house is too quiet again tonight. I used to spend a lot of time wishing it would be quiet. Night after night as I listened to Dad and Mother fighting, I kept hoping they would stop. I used to get scared when they fought. I even tried to stop them once about three years ago. Dad threw me against a wall and I almost passed out. After that Mother and I had one of our talks about Dad's drinking and she ordered me to stay out of the way when they were fighting. That is the only time I can ever remember Mother with her arms around me. I was shaking so much she probably thought she had to hold me still to talk to me.

Sunday, January 19, 1969

Last night I stayed at Karen's and it was fun even if I am tired today. After we were supposed to be in bed, we got out her make-up box and tried on all sorts of faces. We made each other up to look about eighteen. Karen has so many shades of eye shadow, lipstick, nail polish, blusher, and mascara. She doesn't even have to buy them. Her sisters and cousins know how much she loves make-up so they give her the things they get tired of.

It must have been almost midnight when Karen's mother came in. I thought she'd be mad. Mine would have hit the ceiling. I guess it's hard to stay mad while you're laughing. Our faces looked pretty funny by that time. Karen's mother just told us to wash our faces and get some sleep. She even kissed us both goodnight before she left.

Monday, January 20, 1969

What a day! I got a good lead in "Wonderful Town"! I'll be singing two songs all by myself. Miss Jackson will use the men's glee club from the high school in the musical too. She says the junior high is short on men's voices. I think my grades helped me get my lead from Susan Jay. She's a ninth grade who got a smaller part, but everyone thinks she is a better singer.

Friday, February 7, 1969

This is the first day we've had for a long time with no rehearsal. I never realized how much dancing I'd need to do. It's not hard to pick up the steps, but Miss Jackson looks natural doing them and I look stiff. I'll really have to practice if I'm going to look loose for the production. I like being able to stay at school in the afternoons. I wish I didn't have to go home at all. Mother is never home anymore now that Dad is gone and home is the loneliest place in the world.

Sunday, February 23, 1969

Dad has been in prison for exactly a year now and it's all my fault. He wouldn't be there if I had kept my room neat. No one would tell me why he didn't go to a hospital instead of a prison. I only testified so he could get help with his drinking. He kept watching me at the hearing. He couldn't believe that I would tell the court I had been raped. I wish I could take back those words so he would be home.

Mother was furious. I don't think she blamed me for putting Dad in prison. She even said he might be able to be helped there. What had her so mad was that the paper printed the results of the hearing and everyone found out why Dad went to prison. Things like rape should be private.

Practicing my dance steps makes me feel better. When I'm dancing, I can forget about everything else. I don't think I look so stiff anymore. I've been practicing in front of a mirror.

Thursday, February 27, 1969

Debbie is having a slumber party tomorrow night, but I was not invited. I guess she doesn't like having a friend who would send her own father to prison. Ever since Dad went away, Debbie has avoided me. Most of the rest of my friends are used to me again, but I miss Debbie a lot. She used to be a best friend like Karen. Mother says we'll go to a movie tomorrow. She must know how lonely I get on Fridays without rehearsals.

Friday, February 28, 1969

Mother and I went to see "Gone With the Wind" tonight. It was long, but I loved it all. I wanted to cry a few times, but I didn't want Mother to think I was a child so I swallowed a lot and kept in the tears. Mother never cries. Tonight I wanted to be as grown up as she is.

Friday, March 7, 1969

This afternoon when Karen and Debbie and I stopped at Baker Drug, we saw some of the boys from the glee club. Jeff Hilton has the lead opposite mine in the musical, but he is sixteen and never pays any attention to me except during rehearsals so I was surprised to see him and his friends looking at us and laughing. Later Jeff came over and asked me how much longer I was going to try to pass for a seventh grader. To make matters worse, my face got all hot so I couldn't pretend I didn't know what he meant. I don't know what hit me. I just burst into tears and started running as fast as I could go. When I stopped, I found I was at the playground swings.

Karen caught up with me. I could tell she didn't know what to say, but she hugged me for a minute until I stopped crying. We swang for a few minutes and waited for Debbie to find us, but she never came.

Monday, March 17, 1969

I thought maybe Mother was finally going to let me talk to her about Dad tonight, but I was wrong. I was trying to study, but I couldn't concentrate at all. I went into the kitchen for some milk and Mother asked why I wasn't in bed. When I told her I didn't feel tired yet, she started in on the lecture about my being too tired to realize I needed sleep. Before she could tell me the musical was making me over-tired, I asked her how Dad was when she saw him yesterday. She said he was O.K. I told her I missed him. I wanted her to tell me she missed him too, but she didn't. Instead she put on the look that makes her face seem made out of stone. She told me I ought to forget about Dad and that I shouldn't miss him after what he did to me. Then she told me the subject was closed.

Mother just doesn't understand. What Dad did to me was an accident. Mother had warned me what happens to boys when girls take their clothes off. If Dad came home, it could never happen again because I would be so good and keep my room clean. I know I could do it. My room has been clean since the day Dad left. Maybe I can explain it to Mother some other day before she puts on her stone face and says the subject is closed.

Saturday, March 29, 1969

Good morning! I'm sorry to wake you up so early, Journal, but I can't seem to fall asleep. Mother and I just got home from the musical. "Wonderful Town" went very well. There were so many more people in the audience than there were last week. I think the gym was full. You should have heard them clap! That made me feel so good. Afterwards, Miss Jackson told me she was very proud of me. That felt good too.

Mother came backstage later. Everybody was hugging and kissing everyone else. I hoped Mother would hug me, but I should have known better. Mother doesn't touch people. She says it looks cheap in public. In private, times for hugging never seem to come. I felt like she thought I looked cheap when I congratulated other members of the cast. We were about the first people to leave.

Mother took me to Baker Drug for a malt. Mr. Baker has been in and out of the hospital for over a year now. Tonight he looked well and was especially nice to us. He even fixed me an extra dark chocolate malt, himself. Mr. Baker said he was glad the musical was finally over because he had lost most of his after school help to it. I tried to smile, but I wish the musical would never be over.

As we finished our malts, Mother asked me where I had ever learned to dance. I told her I'd practiced a lot in front of her long mirror. She didn't exactly say I shouldn't have learned, but I knew she wasn't proud of me the way Miss Jackson had been.

Sunday, March 30, 1969

Sorry to get you up again, Journal, but you really do help me get sleepy.

The cast party was the biggest party I've ever been to. I danced with a lot of boys I'd never met before. I was beginning to enjoy it until I saw Jeff coming to dance with me. I didn't run this time. It was really strange. He didn't try to talk to me. We just danced. The fast dance turned into a slow one and he held me very tight. It felt safe and I wanted to stay there for a long time. He said he would see me later, but I left before he came back.

Karen and I walked home together. We almost bumped into Susan Jay necking with the boy she has been dating during the musical. If I were a ninth grader, maybe I would be dating a boy too.

Thursday, April 17, 1969

Today we had to write a story in English. Usually I enjoy writing stories, but today I couldn't think of a single thing I dared to write about. I dreamed about Dad last night and my head was still full of him. I knew I had to be careful or something awful might come out of my pen. I finally wrote a few paragraphs about a monkey. It seemed safer than trying to write about people. It was a terrible composition. Miss May will be disappointed. So was I.

Monday, April 21, 1969

Miss May handed back all the compositions except for mine. Since we have English before lunch, I had time to stop at her desk on the way out. Like an idiot, I mentioned the missing composition. She told me she had lost it. I was so surprised and relieved, I started to cry. I gulped in a lot of air and tried to stop, but I couldn't. I was really out of control. She handed me some Kleenex and told me to go ahead and cry. She said I shouldn't try to keep all my feelings inside me. For a minute I was afraid she would want to know what was wrong, but she didn't ask any questions. She just put her arms around me and held me until the tears went away. Before I left, I told her I was glad she had lost my composition. She smiled and looked at me like I was her friend instead of just her student. I think I fell a little bit in love with Miss May this noon. What's wrong with me, Journal? Girls aren't supposed to fall in love with women.

Saturday, April 26, 1969

Mother was shopping today when the doorbell rang. Jeff Hilton was standing on our front porch grinning at me. I was so glad to see a friendly face, I invited him in for a Coke. We talked and he said that he really wanted to take me out. I told him I would not be old enough to date for another year. He said we could go for a walk this afternoon. It didn't have to be a date.

We walked for such a long time that I lost track of where we were. It looked like we were in the country. It was like a dream. He took my hands and helped me climb rocks and trees. He lifted me down from branches and walked with his arm around my shoulder. He even kissed me lots of times. I knew I should not let him because I'm not old enough to date yet. I knew Mother would think he was cheap. I guess I must be cheap too.

Jeff started to unbutton my shirt, but I wouldn't let him. He asked what I was afraid of and told me I had the nicest figure he had ever seen on a girl. I said we'd better go back. I didn't know when Mother would be home. I told Jeff Mother liked me to be with friends who are my own age. When he asked if I told my mother whom she could be with, I was surprised. He said the whole world knew my mother was having an affair with Mr. Baker. I could tell I was going to cry so I started to run, but I couldn't see where I was going and, besides, I was still lost. When Jeff caught up to me, I wanted to tell him he was lying, but I knew he wasn't.

He could tell I didn't feel like talking on the way home. We were just quiet together again like the night at the dance. Mother wasn't home when we got there. Jeff said he wanted me to go walking with him again next Saturday. I felt really mad at Mother and I said yes.

Tonight I had a hard time talking to Mother, but she did not notice. She told me she had been invited to spend tomorrow with some friends near the prison. I told her to have a good time. I hope she finds time to visit Dad.

Wednesday, April 30, 1969

For some reason I've thought more about Mother and Mr. Baker this week than I have about Jeff. I guess I've been thinking about Dad too. If Mother was having an affair with Mr. Baker, maybe she wanted Dad to go away. Was that why she wanted me to testify against him? I thought Mother wanted to help Dad. . . . I don't think I want to write anymore, Journal.

Thursday, May 1, 1969

Tonight Mother came into my room and asked me how well I knew Jeff Hilton. I told her I knew him from the cast of "Wonderful Town" and that we went walking together last Saturday. She blew up—something about cheap theater friends. I wondered how she'd found out about Jeff and me so soon. When she calmed down enough so I could understand her again, she told me if I was going to be a whore, I'd need some pills. I tried to tell her we hadn't done anything like that, but she wouldn't believe me. She threw a box of little white pills at me and told me to take one every day until they were gone.

Then she started yelling about my reputation. By this time I was mad too so I asked her why she didn't worry about hers instead. Before she could answer, I told her I knew about her affair with Mr. Baker and I thought she liked Mr. Baker better than Dad and that was why she'd made me send Dad to prison. Mother stared at me for a minute and then she slapped me harder than ever before, but she didn't say it wasn't true. All I wanted her to do was tell me it wasn't true. She didn't even try to tell me it wasn't true.

Saturday, May 3, 1969

This afternoon Jeff brought a car and we drove a long way before we started our walk. Jeff said he was sorry about last week. He thought I'd known about my mother. I told him I guessed I had.

Today's walk was like last week's. We ran and climbed and kissed. It was almost like being a child again. We had started earlier so it wouldn't be over so soon. Jeff took me back to the car where he got out a blanket, some sandwiches, and some warm Coke. We took them to a little clearing surrounded by bushes and had a picnic. After we ate, we necked. I wanted Jeff to hug me some more so when he started to unbutton my shirt, I let him. I was shaking by the time he had taken off my bra, but then he put my shirt back on without it and I wasn't so nervous. He kept touching my breasts for the longest time. It made me want to hug him harder. We lay down together and I knew what he would want to do next.

I felt really scared when Jeff helped me take off my slacks. He took off more of his clothes, but while I was trying to watch Jeff, I kept seeing Dad. Jeff told me not to worry about babies because he was protected. I wasn't worried about babies. Dad hadn't given me one. It didn't hurt much this time and I didn't even want to get sick, but I still can't see what is so great about going all the way. Maybe it is the only way a girl can get hugged and kissed.

Mother told me if I ever let a boy go all the way with me on a date, he would lose respect for me and never take me out again. She was wrong. Before Jeff said good-bye, he said he'd come back again next Saturday.

Thursday, May 8, 1969

Things at home have been a little tense this week, but Mother does not usually come home until after I'm asleep and with school, we haven't spent much time trying to talk. We watch each other a lot. I think we both want to talk again, but we don't know what to say. Mother looks like she's expecting something terrible to happen. I feel like she is afraid of me. Jeff will be here again on Saturday. I can't understand why Mother hasn't told me not to see him anymore. I really thought she would.

Saturday, May 10, 1969

Jeff got here before noon and this time I brought the sandwiches and cold Cokes. It was so great to see him again.

We got to our clearing and he held me in his arms for a long time. We ate before the Coke got warm. This time we never even went for a walk.

Jeff said he was going to make love to me today so that I would enjoy it just as much as he did. We necked very slowly. By the time we got around to the last part, I would have known how to do it even if it had never happened before. I finally found out why people like making love. Jeff says I'm good at it. Making love is the first thing I've been good at for a very long time.

A DREAM

Sallou Cole

Anger falls
solid anchors
on page
intent
on wind
clanking wheels
sounding just
against
restrained screams
tired screams
called out
a trace in
still air
fighting
i dream of them
pounding
against your
flesh, rape
smothering
i cant reach
you cant see
me, hear me
calling
damn
police, men
that will take
you away
feed you drugs
to calm defenses
rape again
only worse
this time

they go for
your mind
(dont they ever stop?)
still wrestling
you cannot forget
his eyes cock
vivid forced
upon your resisting
flesh
moaning, spitting
everywhere you
see him, doctor
cop, rapist . . .
i watch them take
you away, frantic
you cant see me
it is only a dream
it continues
awake
hands lock
against darkness
footsteps
out there
damn men
in every street
and alley
        waiting . . .
        awake
     why couldnt i
       help you
      hold you
      protect you
      awake
haunted by their
madness
haunted by your
pain

come to me
　i cannot face
this alone
i dream another
dream
fighting protection
from mens weapons
and chains
i dream of mountains
at the edge of the
city, where we
scream hungry
for the mothers
bleeding
beyond the pain
beyond the last cord
we make more
thicker ones
bound tightly
sealed
bones digging
down into
the earth

Lark d'Helen

There's nothing so strange about my family. We kids came in pairs. The two older kids (8 and 9 years older than me), my brother and myself (he is 3 years younger), and the two "little" kids (8 and 9 years younger than me). Dad was a minister in a very conservative, fundamental church. Mom was a pastor's wife who didn't fit the mold; she was too creative, too "emotional."

We laughed a lot in my family, and we yelled a lot. Mom and Dad had money problems, church problems, teenagers and babies—and us middle kids were just kind of in there some where.

As far back as I can remember . . . is my older brother, Alan, laughing at me—and touching me. I can't untangle the loving from the not loving. He was my "big brother." He made special things for me. He taught me to ride my bike. He defended me against other kids. He touched my body and looked at me naked. He made mock of me a lot. I liked being loved, but then it would become something else. Remembering is a deathly menstrual cramp squeezing the life and love out of me.

I don't remember when my brother-in-law, Bob, started touching me; maybe I was nine. I often stayed at my sister's house. For a while they lived with our family and in high school I lived with them for two years. During the time I lived with them, I told my boyfriend about Bob's touching me and coercing me. My boyfriend went to our house and beat Bob up, chased him around the neighborhood yelling things. My sister picked me up from school. She never warned me. We turned the corner and there were all the police cars, with their red lights flashing, the blood all over, the questions, the pastor with his bible, my boyfriend, the neighbors. My God, I can't stand to remember the pain. It was covered up. I agreed that I had lied. Bob's touching, getting into bed with me, never stopped.

The next time I told someone was when Bob was staying with my husband and me. I asked Roger not to leave me alone with Bob. He laughed.

I had bladder and kidney problems most of my life, but mostly I didn't tell anyone when I was really in pain. At age 28 the discomfort and inconvenience forced the decision to check it out. The doctor connected it with the childhood sexual abuse. I had to deal with my past.

BOB,

Do you ever think about the things you did to me and the agony it has caused me? The agony it is causing me? Well, I do! And I think it's about time you put your mind to it too!

I don't remember the first time you touched me—but I remember a lot of other times. I remember a time in the house on Rose Road. I was in fourth grade—pretty young, don't you think? You sucked on my clitoris and put your tongue in my vagina. Afterwards you went in the bathroom. I wondered why. To jack off, maybe? I remember your pulling me down on the bed and kissing me and feeling me while Maggie was cooking supper during one of my summer stays with you. I remember your coming home from a trip in Orlando and cornering me in my bedroom, feeling me up. Maggie's hair was a mess the next morning and she told me proudly that her husband had been home last night. I knew you'd gotten hot with me, and I felt like shit! I remember when you came home from being in the delivery room with Maggie and climbed in bed with me. I despised you, but I had never been taught that I could say no to you.

Why the hell were you so worried about my dating habits when I stayed with you? You'd already taught me plenty yourself.

Do you know, Bob Gray, that I could have had you arrested for first degree sexual assault? One to twenty years for that—which is a lot shorter than the time I'm putting in for your fun. The chronic urethral infections and recurring bladder scar tissue I have are direct results of your and Alan's playing around and my reluctance (because of guilt) to tell anyone of my pain in that area of my body. Every time I take a pill and every time I'm catheterized and go through that demeaning procedure I hate your guts!

Do you have any idea the mind trip you laid on me? Obviously you knew I wouldn't fight back—I'd been taught in the good Baptist tradition that a person (and especially a girl) should always respect her elders, particularly men. What was I supposed to do? I trusted you; you were the adult, I was the kid. And, sure, it felt good—my body's normal. Then, of course, I was also full of the teachings that men only seduce women (and children) because women "flirt." I grew up with a huge guilt complex—you should have been living with it all these years.

I also had to deal with sexual feelings that couldn't be acknowledged—that were "sinful." But you put them there. Being a teenager was the pits! I needed boyfriends—to fill the sexual desires you gave me—but I hated them—like I hated you for what you did to me. I still hate you for that!

That time in Orlando—you knew the mind trip I was going through—did you care? NO!!! You saved your own skin at my expense. How did you know that if you lied I would back you up? Only because you knew the terrible bind I was in. You knew I had no support for telling the truth. You knew my only means of survival was to agree with your lie. Did it feel good to destroy a person, a kid? You killed my sister's love for you—did that feel good? You're damn lucky I didn't commit suicide. Then what would you have told people? But you really didn't worry about that—you knew I'd been brought up a good Christian, that I would take a good share of the guilt on myself, that I would feel that I was supposed to suffer because I was so sinful.

Bob, how often you have played the pious act on me. You're holier than I! How I hate you for that routine. Over my marriage, over Ann's baby. I've despised you more each year—each year that you went on not even caring about what you did to me but growing more "Christian."

Did you have to go through the trauma that I went through when I got married? How could I trust the man I married? My experiences, thanks to you, had been rotten so far. More than not meeting my needs you were a destructive force in my life.

Each time I have to deal with the emotional, sexual and physical problems you left me with, I think about you. And the more I think, the more you make me sick to my stomach!

TO MY MOTHER,

Stop! Listen to ME! Hear my experience. I am angry that you wouldn't hear me in the past. And even now as we talk of my pain, your response is to protect the men with such statements as "they may have changed," "it happened a long time ago," "what's the purpose in bringing it all up," "those poor men, with such cold wives." Why?! Am I worth so much less than they? They were protected when I was young, I was not. And now again, you are protecting them, rather than me. You are worried about my upsetting their lives. Have you considered how they have upset mine? Why do I have to "prove" that the effect on my life is bad *enough* to face them with it? By openly acknowledging their actions upon me I am not wrecking or even damaging their lives. They did that when they abused me. I have been covering for them all these years. I have been paying. I am not "doing" to them, they "did" to me!

How could I talk to you when I was small? You wouldn't believe me! If I didn't like someone's touching me, you told me I was silly, or fussy, or something like that. I didn't have the right to not like touching unless I could prove it was bad. I had to prove I was truthful in order to be believed rather than being believed until I was proven untruthful. It is still that way. You questioned me until you believed that the abuse I took was really as bad as I claim. You couldn't just believe me. Now I can answer most of your questions, but then I couldn't. At first I didn't know why I didn't like the touching. Later I felt too guilty and ashamed to try to understand, even to myself, why I was both attracted and repelled by their touching.

How could I tell you I didn't like my brother to hug me? I'm supposed to love my brother. All the stories I grew up on were about brothers and sisters—loving each other, always being loyal to each other, and the family, always protecting each other. I was taught to show my love for God by loving others, and to me others meant my brothers and sisters particularly.

You tell me that I shouldn't talk to anyone in the family that doesn't already know. But that is one of the principles that set me up for this abuse—each keeping our own little secrets. It is one reason why you, my mother, weren't told about the incident in Orlando. We were all keeping our own little secrets, even if it killed us. We built a false reality that removed the possibility of drawing support and protection from others in the family.

It has not just now started bothering me. It has always hurt me, but before no one else knew it. Am I wrong for owning my pain honestly? NO! Unless a person admits that it's snowing, she isn't going to shovel the walk. Well, our family doesn't get a lot of walks shovelled, and I've got a lot of snow drifted over this one! I'm trying to dig myself out. Mom, I've always had physical and emotional problems; I am simply belatedly dealing with problems, problems left to me by others.

When I was a child you often commented on how "touchy" I was. I always wanted to be hugged, or held, or touched somehow. You chose to say that it was just my "sensitive personality." How I hated that! How I still do hate that! That view not only "excused" my behavior but also discredited my whole reality.

Mom, I don't understand how you could do that to me. You have fought such labels all your life also. You were always too creative, too intelligent, too alive to fit the mold that women in our sphere were supposed to fit. Were you trying to make me fit where you couldn't? Maybe you thought that by forcing me to fit the mold I would have an easier life than you did. Maybe you thought other things, I don't know. But I couldn't fit the mold! And you wouldn't hear me.

Hear me now! I love you.

HETERO

Donna Levreault

Where it begins
between dark and light
the embrace of child green
you as the two of us.
I smooth away the smoke, the dew
and see clearly the one
as two.
you yellow/pink
cave blossom born into my arms
out of the clay of night
I mother/red
lightening black
diving down under
I bury deeper into you
wondering what I have created.

The bells   the sea   the cries
you are my father
tossing in a heap of nightmares
ashen/struck motionless
beneath the waves
Out of your mouth the foreign life
unsexed and convulsing into horror
You came out of me
but I don't know you
The black pit opens and you say
I have caused all this terror
to be unleashed and
all these mad dogs to pull at your flesh
You say I planned it this way
that my desire has torn away
the very fabric of your being

You are my father
but I return to you as my lover
Out of me you came
shaped from the clay of this night
yellow/pink
underbelly of whales
we merge together
and the tide pushes me
closer to this thing I have made.

The explosion   the splitting   the swirling
You are my brother
beady eyes pressed to the crack
of my door
You are the dark wooden one
I've refused as kin
and I chase you away
into your own corner
I wrap the cobwebs tightly around your face
and you groan
A horrible mutant shape appears
a plant form I've never seen
Out of me you came
but I don't know you
Black hole of a mouth
You say
you have never known the gold
or the silver of love
that you have remained a voyeur
rather than a true explorer of passion.
You say I shut the door
when you needed to know
how two becomes one
and then two again.
You are my brother
but I return to you as my lover

yellow/pink
pools of hidden honey
You came out of me
but now I return
and come out of you
lover   brother   father
red/mother
black lightening
Pulling me down   down   down
away from the breakers of dawn
down into the silent moving
shadows of an alien world.

MOTHER, LOVE

Robyn Wiegman

You empty into me
in a dream
over the awful salts of a woman
you would watch grow until

until your eyes blackened in shame.
Yes, I have found you here
this night washed in the water
you made me in,
smiling in the brine clear light
of a life lived touching
and not in fear.
Always I wanted the wet lips
of your secret cave, the map
that draws me to it.

Out of the dream, I know
things were better when
we were one,
my thimble self tucked alive
in your womb, our breath
a single sigh.
You loved me as yourself.

Mother, did you never expect me
to understand this loin hunger
for my own flesh,
did you never think
I would remember.

LETTER

Lee Ann Schlaf

Initially my memories were very vague and dream like. Flashes would come back to me as I was in a pre-dream state or some other relaxed setting.

I remember being in class at school. We were doing a relaxation exercise. In the middle of a peaceful field of waist-high wheat I saw something very strange . . . I saw myself as a little girl dressed in a red snow suit in the house where I grew up. I'm standing on a dining room chair as my father dresses me for winter in Chicago. He begins to fondle my genitals. I want him to stop . . . I feel paralyzed . . . I can't stop him. I'm three years old and I don't like my dad much. He's unpredictable, easily angered and only occasionally touches me . . . What an awful image! I'd like to just let that one pass! But I'm too curious to let it go at that. I describe the image of the snow suit to my mother in detail to affirm my memory. She says "yes, why do you ask?"

A couple of weeks later as I'm falling asleep another unpleasant picture comes to mind. This time my mother and I are both naked in the house. We're walking from room to room but keep being pushed to the floor by a large penis. I wake up crying and scared. Luckily I am sleeping with a caring lover. He holds me and listens to my fears.

I think it was at this point that I felt I really needed to explore these "strange" thoughts and what they might mean. I had a setting to do this since I was in primal therapy at the time.

My therapist told me to focus on feelings and not to worry about actual events. I was able to do that. In doing that I uncovered many hurtful memories of my father's sexual expressions toward me. I found a way to explore some of the rage I felt at wanting affection and not getting it. The confusion I felt about whose fault it was and that I had somehow done something wrong. I felt sadness and anger at my mother for not being there for me and not recognizing my little girl signals for help. I was afraid of the dark. Afraid to be left alone. Desperate when she would want to go out and leave me alone with Dad. Fearful of being hurt by some "stranger" and screaming out in the night from "bad dreams."

Guilt. Somehow the guilty finger gets pointed at the victim in cases of rape or incest. It's only recently that I have felt clear enough about all of this to tell a few trusted friends. Now I can see that the sexual contact I had with my father was *not* my fault. Somehow the message comes across; the woman (child) could have prevented it. Or it happened because the child (woman) wanted it to and was seductive. Sure I wanted love, attention and touch. What child doesn't? But that was very different from what I got! I was hurt, controlled, lied to, denied and threatened with *more* abuse if I told. This was a secret that I was told to discuss with no one. Finally, it was implied I had asked for this. That was nothing like the love and tenderness I was wanting when I smiled at or was flirtatious with my father.

I am in therapy now and find that my relationship with my dad has definitely affected how I view the world. In exploring my feelings about our contact I've found keys to how I feel about myself, my body, relating to men and women and how capable I feel in the world. It has been vital that I have had a safe place to talk about the pain and confusion I have felt. It has been wonderful to do therapy with a person who is able to really hear me. She has helped me see the problem of incest in a larger context. She recommended a book, *Conspiracy of Silence/The Trauma of Incest* by Sandra Butler. This was helpful in giving me more facts about this common but unspoken family problem.

It has been about five years now since I first began to look at my feelings about all of this. I don't think I am finished yet sorting it all out. But I do find that the more I speak about it the more clarity and strength I feel.

TO DADDY

Tracy Nagurski

I

it's time.
to reclaim my childhood,
my past
that in your sickness you took from me.
for protection
it has hid its horrors;
the terror
disconnected—but never far from me
speaks itself in anxiety and powerlessness.
the shame
wears your name,
not mine.
      i give back to you your darkness.

II

i promised you i wouldn't tell
anyone
anything.
anything
to make you go away.
then you went away for good
and i kept my promise
by burying my childhood with you—
buried so far down
it transformed itself
into a dull, nagging ache.
later, i began to cry.
and i cried

a long time,
always to my lovers,
trying to pin it on them.
they didn't understand
where my pain was coming from—
i didn't understand
and thought i was crazy.

slowly
painfully
i unburied me
then you
and the nagging ache
is now a torrent;
my insides
turbulent,
raging.
and simultaneously
my world crumbles
and comes together
with the breaking of that promise.

III

you taught me so well
to hate myself,
my body,
that i don't need you anymore
to hurt me,
fuck me physically
or emotionally.
i do very well on my own now.
and the voice of that hatred
sounds so much like mine
it's hard to believe
that once i was a

live
loving
child/person
who never would have dreamed
of cutting her arms
just to feel the pain
and watch her blood run.

MY DEAR SISTER NANCY,

Susan Marie Norris
(Cygnet)

How I wish for another reason to write. Some simple joyful event. Instead, after attempting this in familiar ways: in mind, with pen, revising endlessly, I choose a new tack, to freely share my pain of letting go of what we could have been. My first fear says, "You might seem crazy. Control to be logical. Do not let her see your raw pain."

I have told you I am an incest victim. What I have not said is you are too, as is our entire family. I've gone to Christopher Street for treatment beginning last June and am still in an aftercare group.

As a result of opening all of my doors on our family's secrets, I have confronted my destructive behaviors: chemical dependency, self-hate, guilt, compulsiveness, withdrawing from people, worrying, perfectionism, undereating, procrastination, over-scheduling, no play time, setting up people to be angry, not enough sleep, abusive relationships, using coffee and sugar to avoid dealing with my feelings, too high expectations of myself, not being assertive, not owning my worth, blaming, keeping secrets, overwork, staying a victim, lack of exercise, denial, not taking my space, abstaining from sex, giving up my power, ignorance about my body, learning the hard way, being reckless while driving and having accidents, accumulating traffic tickets, and using contraceptives irresponsibly. I've taken responsibility for what is mine and let go of my shame.

When we last talked on the phone because you were too angry to see me, you could only blame me for hurting Mother and Dad. I had hoped to see you then, but you took their side. Our parents have abused me over and over for the forty-two years of my life. What I have done is to take my power back, and stop letting them do it. They declare they love me, but they hate that I am a lesbian. They had nothing to say when I told them Uncle Harold sexually abused me. I asked them why they hadn't protected me since they knew he had done the same to you and they said nothing. That's abusive. I respect myself. I make mistakes, but I am a person deserving of love and respect. Saying what's true is more important than keeping quiet to my family.

Nancy. Nancy. Nancy. I mourn for us. We are casualties. We are victims. We talk to each other of loving sisters. Needing closeness with one person. One possible person in our family. Our words travel back, toward Minneapolis and Los Angeles. We have struggled to do something different towards each other: my trips up the back stairs when you were living newly married on the third floor of our house in Kenwood. The proud grand house on Irving Avenue "with the third floor for Nancy. And John." You were twenty, I was eleven. There you made me grilled cheese sandwiches and tomato soup. (Mother said he was beating you then. And I kept the secret.)

Trips to Lake Minnetonka, where you lived in three or four different houses. One sunny June afternoon in 1952, I came to see you, with the boy who loved me, and to swim. You were not home. I don't remember your comforting me while we waited for the men with their grappling hooks to catch his free, limp, too heavy for me to hold body. You took me, what you thought was me, to a neighbor's house where we sat in their kitchen "making conversation." But I had left. I was not in the house. I was in the lake holding Roger, and in the boat looking for Roger to appear, to be saved in time. (I did not say that to you. I kept my secret.)

Trips to Los Angeles and on to West Covina where you were continuing to live as a minister's wife, a mother, a nice person, a pretty woman, a person everyone had told me all my life I should be like . . .

"Why can't you be like Nancy?"   Mother
"Why aren't you like Nancy?"   Lake Harriet School
    Teachers
"Why aren't you Nancy?"   Bob Jones University
    Faculty

The first trip to you, living across from your church in West Covina, when I was twenty-one. This was my graduation present from college—from our parents.

"Send her away so she will be apart from him."   Mother
"She'll forget all about Ivan."   Mother
"You will be glad you broke your engagement when
    you're away."   Mother
"You crazy girl! How could you have done this to me.
    Choosing a rough Canadian who is ignorant. He doesn't
    fit into OUR WAY OF LIFE!"   Mother's thoughts

I took the ticket. I had no plans now that I had no husband to follow. I took their present—their ticket—her ticket—my ticket—my trip. I came for a visit and stayed at least a month. You took care of me. You took me in with no questions. You had written me a long letter I have saved saying, "Don't do it. Don't marry him. You're blind now. I can see this. Don't trust yourself. Trust me." You took care of me, Nancy. I wasn't sick with the mumps or the whooping cough or the flu or the measles or the chicken pox. I was sick with the knowledge that I had been blind. I didn't know what to do with a B.A. in English and no teaching certificate. I had no plans. You made me grilled cheese sandwiches and tomato soup. (I hear him yelling at you and knew he had beaten you. And I kept your secret.)

Memories: your pinning me on the livingroom floor on Ewing Avenue tickling me until I cried. I screamed. I choked. I couldn't breathe. Holding me down. Doing it to me over and over. Raping me over and over. Feeling endless panic and helplessness. Powerlessness.

Memories: starting around the corner at night up the stairs to my bedroom. You, jumping out at me screaming a noise. Me jumping inside myself. Outside myself. Feelings of terror, panic, helplessness. Powerlessness. Never, after those times, going up a flight of stairs to my room, however old, without the fantasy, "Someone will come from behind and rape me." Looking around, over my shoulder. Keeping on going.

Memories: racing in a wagon down a dusty hill at Mound, our cottage we loved, you pulling me. You tripping or letting go somehow. Me going to crash, to go into a wreck. You scared, having to tell Mother. Me bloody. Feelings of terror, panic, and helplessness. Powerlessness.

Memories: taken to "Club," your high school club. "Why do I have to take her?" to Mother. Sitting off to the side watching you, watching them watching me. Knowing you hated me, you hated me there. Being in a strange house with a group of strangers. Your friends. All of them hating me. More than once we went together. You hating me. Me hating me. Me hating you. (I knew we hated each other, and I kept our secret.)

Memories: me below you in my bottom iron bunk bed on the back screened-in porch at Mound, our cottage we loved, pushing you up on your mattress, letting go, hearing you laugh, hearing the bed squeak. Having fun at night.

Memories: your bicycle, blue. Now mine. Racing it. Beating all of my friends. Riding miles, after we moved again, to see Margaret. Loving it because it was yours. Being given your clothes when you unpacked your black trunk from college. Going to the same college in South Carolina. Joining the same sorority. Having your black metal trunk to put my clothes in. My clothes—your clothes—my clothes. My life—your life—my life. (I knew I was still trying to be like you, and I kept it secret.)

Your memories: "Why don't you remember any good times, Susan? I remember when you were small

> You were held
> You were loved
> You were cute
> Everybody loved you
> You were everybody's little girl
> I showed you off
> You talked and people laughed
> Your babytalk was so funny
> You were held
> Dad held you
> Mother held you
> I held you
> You were loved
> You were spoiled
> Dad loved you. He read you the funnies on his lap even
>   when you could read

Don't you remember? Why don't you remember? Trust me. Don't trust yourself. I'm sane. I'm eight and a half years older. You're crazy. You're the baby " (I couldn't remember those early years. Knowing that frightened me, and I kept that secret.)

Your trips to me: feeling together, feeling even. More even than ever before. Your coming for the folks' fiftieth wedding anniversary. Your coming to be my matron of honor that September ten years ago. Your coming to Sun City three years ago to be with me at our parents' house. Good times. Rich times.

Your calls to me: saying this was instead of the letters you didn't write. Saying you felt guilty for not writing. Saying you loved me. You were "in my corner."

My calls to you: many. Money. Freely spent to talk with the one person whom I thought was there for me. Asking to borrow five hundred dollars on my first house. Hearing you ask, "Why not more? I have more. It's o.k. You're o.k."

Racing. My memories. Until this moment. Stop. I have arrived. Caught up. I have said all of the past that is important to recall, retell, relive. I will tell you the truth about now. I think you may be chemically dependent. You do not support me. You are afraid of me. I have to let you go. I want a relationship with you and I am not going to do any more of the work but say that. The rest is yours.

UNTITLED INCEST PIECE

Anne Lee

I woke up writing the incest thing, which is predictably garbled and not fiction, and so oblique as to be ridiculous, which is maybe the point, and resolved or not, one hesitates to stir things up, and one writes without verbs, as though that matters, and without motion of any kind, and what one says is my father my brother my father my brother, and having moved past the oblivion and pain, past the hate and anger, one is astonished to feel nothing at all. Which raises, I suppose, a lot of questions, and makes one feel that maybe the real telling is impossible after all, and the verbless telling not useful, perhaps, or to be desired, and yet one has begun, however badly, the telling, and so, must need go on. To write about it, I suppose, is to readmit the shame, which returns the anger and resurrects the pain, so that one is back at the beginning as though nothing has changed—no work been done, no wounds been healed. To write it down, I suppose, is to resurrect the child who wet herself in terror and screamed and screamed and screamed. To resurrect the child who feared and hated and would have killed, and gladly, who remembered nothing but the hate and fear, and kept herself awake at night by reading, a pattern she retains as souvenir. To write about it is to conjure up the adolescent, still fearful, still reading, her back to the wall, eating herself into immunity, defending herself with such weapons as come to hand. To write about it is to uncover and expose the young woman, raped repeatedly by her own paralysis, by her residual terrors, by her intimate knowledge of the inevitable, by her understanding of the unspeakable and her desire to escape it.

There were names for none of this when she was young, and her life was accepted for what it was, and she knew nothing and accepted everything, and assumed that that was how it was. To be a child, an adolescent, a young woman. She was unaware of her behavior, her patterns, her pain, and did not, until later, attribute them to their real causes. Her anger was bad, her reading was bad, her fear and pain and screams were bad, and brought with them punishments of their own, and if there had been names for those parts of her life, she would still have remained silent, because there was nothing and no one to tell. Nothing to tell which would not destroy her in ways more terrible than this. Nothing to tell which, if somehow articulated, would be believed. Nothing to tell.

It was years before she found names for her anger and words for her pain, and she shouted them all at once and felt better, and whispered them softly and felt ashamed, and repeated them slowly until they had been absorbed and could be put away again, and she helped others find the words she had found for herself, and watched them grow stronger as she had done, but when she began to write about it, she burst at last into tears.

So much for process.

What I say about incest, is that it could happen to anybody, and probably has.

What one does with incest, is to compress it, to make it tiny, make it small; to fit it into the smallest space possible, after eliminating the details. Incest victims, like victims of anything, are without detail. Years of the unspeakable remain unspoken, and I am no exception. Whatever detail there is, is part accident, part defiance, and not intended, ever, to illuminate anything. The purpose of talking about incest is not to illuminate anything, but simply to *say*, to know on another level, and in another way, what has happened.

The incest victim is now frequently billed as a survivor, but to speak in this context, of survival, is to grant to those atrocities a bigger place than one can safely handle. To speak of survival is to admit that there have been, all along, other choices—that one's survival has not necessarily been assured. To speak, in this context, of survival, is to explode more than the myth; it is to destroy simultaneoulsy the created space and the lies which have thus far sustained us. It wasn't really that bad. It could have been worse.

Disclaimers aside, one writes to a friend, and considers form, and sees that however it happens, this telling will emerge in fits and starts, in poetry and prose, in song and dance, in sickness and in health, examined from every conceivable angle, impaled on the head of its pin. There will be solitary murmurs and conversations and hints thrown out, not coyly, and the scraps will be gathered one by one and sewn privately together, and we shall see what we shall see.

Labeling the scraps, then, is the hardest, and arranging them. Labeling and sorting. Putting the scraps in boxes, in places of their own, with others of their kind. Labeling the boxes.

The box of details is empty, still, and likely to remain so, but the box of consequences is bulging, and there is a box for feelings—its contents predictable and large, and a box of implications, whose contents must be examined in light of the contents of the other boxes. The Naming, then. The Sorting. The Consequences.

1. I am not a heavy sleeper.
2. I have never liked tall men.
3. I do not see my brother.
4. I sleep with a light on, or not at all.
5. I am not close to male relatives.
6. I sleep facing my lover.
7. I do not fool around in bathtubs, and much prefer showers.
8. I do not make love in the dark.
9. I sleep very little, and would prefer to sleep in the morning, than at night.
10. My sense of hearing is exceptionally acute.
11. I am unusually startled by sudden noises, and given to jumping.

Some of the consequences of incest which I have overcome with varying degrees of success include:

1. Nightmares
2. Sleepwalking
3. Bedwetting
4. Insomnia
5. Overeating (goal directed)
6. Lying
7. Running away from home
8. Death wish
9. Unwanted pregnancy
10. Chronic depression
11. Helplessness
12. Drinking
13. Doping
14. Marriage
15. Rage
16. Suicidal tendencies
17. Low self esteem
18. Hopelessness
19. Relationships with men
20. Guilt
21. Shame
22. Isolation
23. Terror

And one is a good, if not a better, person, and one has indeed survived one's victimization, and one adds the fact to the list of one's accomplishments, without thinking about it more than is necessary, and it is there, but no longer central. It is there, but no longer a critical part of my definition of myself.

What happened to me could have happened to anybody, and often did, and what I am able, now, to share of that experience, is evidence of my strength and the strength of those who love me.

To recognize and name and then expose the beast, is to move from rage to revolution—to begin at the beginning, the often painful process of survival.

I have, I see, made lists, which are clear, and timely, and to the point, but the separate items even now, from the distance of either paragraphs or years, call forth more words and images, more memory and pain than would have seemed possible only minutes before. For each item, there are words and pages, threatening always to surface, *offering,* perhaps, to surface, yielding up their separate stories, exploding the several, separate cannons of their several, separate lives.

Think what it means, for example, to be "given to jumping." For me, I suppose, those words contain all the blank and unexplicated terror of the original violations, and if the jumping is inconvenient or obtrusive (from time to time), it is, at least, quiet. Quiet is important. It is important to be quiet. It is important to lie still. It is important to be silent, to keep the secrets, to preserve the lies.

The effect of all this silence, is to obscure the facts; to effectively silence the evidence and to deny that parts of one's personality have evolved, not out of conscious choice, but of necessity. The list of consequences of my incest experience which appears here, is the result of 15 years of struggle, and each item on it represents a series of separate and often painful revelations—15 years of light bulbs laid end to end, lighting and relighting themselves at will, precipitated by panic.

The held breath. The baited breath—the one attempt at control. The rigidity of terror, suspended but absorbed. The multiplicity of triggers.

One's own experience is blurred or sometimes obliterated, by time, by the inevitability of years, so that the things or people or events which trigger the old responses are so obscure as to remain unidentified. There is in each of us, a line of little girls, folded and folded like so many paper dolls—each with her separate memories, each with her separate fears. With adulthood comes the advantage of physical size, so that it becomes difficult to remember how small one was. How small and immobilized and dependent and afraid. How one's life depended on one's oppressor, how the messages of love and terror became impossibly entwined, and how the child's hatred and fear were continually discounted, continually misnamed, continually repressed and denied and juggled and condemned.

The crime of incest, like the crime of rape, like the crime of battering, carries with it, always, the threat of death. The child's opportunities for observation are far from legion: she believes what she is told, or she rejects it as best she can, but she has nothing to put in its place. If she believes anything, it is that her life depends on her silence. If she believes anything else, she believes that she is powerless; that to name the beast is not to destroy *it*, but to destroy herself and her family—to explode, forever, the myths of hearth and home—to obliterate, in short, the only game in town.

Her belief in her own potential for destruction is alternately a source of terror and of comfort, providing, as it occasionally does, the illusion of power, the possibility of control. It is also, however, a source of ongoing agony, which necessitates super-human efforts at control which may last a lifetime. There is always the chance that she will speak of it in anger or in despair, that she will, in a moment of rage or weakness, allude to the unspeakable, the unspoken, the unheard of, the unbelievable, the unacceptable, the unreal. There is always the chance that she will betray herself unwittingly, that she will implode upon herself, that she will somehow upset the balance which she has so carefully maintained.

Beside the silence and the imperative of control, there loom the spectres of amnesia and denial, which feed and reinforce each other, and cushion, however slightly, the worst of blows. Selective amnesia is usually a process of blocking the worst, and denying the rest; a process which seeks to remove the cause without ever dealing with its effects. Insofar as she is successful in deluding herself, the incest victim is estranged from her feelings and can only perceive them as invalid in light of the complexities of rationale she has created for herself. Despite, or more properly, *because* of this estrangement, she has only herself to blame, and the circle of guilt is completed. If something happened, something bad, then it must be her fault. If *nothing* happened, then why is she like this? Why does she conform so closely to a pattern of whose existence she is scarecely even aware?

Silent or not, she accepts the guilt, and buries it as best she can, watching it surface from time to time, and feeling it always at her core. As an adult, the myth of complicity reinforces her guilt, and unable either to forget or forgive, her anger remains turned inward upon herself. As an adult, her growing strength and size and independence make it increasingly difficult to recall the extent of her former helplessness, so that she is compelled to assume the additional guilt of her failure to prevent her own violations.

As an adult, she knows that what is rape for a woman, is incest for a child. When it's your father or your brother. When the rapist loves you, or says he does, or you know he's supposed to love you. So what is rape for a woman is incest for a child. Or molestation. The words themselves serve to trivialize her experience, and the semantic lines define it further, as something which happens to *children,* rather than as something which happened to the child she used to be. The distinctions here are reason enough to deter her from the opening of old wounds, for to do so, is not only to precipitate pain willingly, but to return to the state of childhood. To remember, is to regress—to remove the careful, clanking armor of adulthood, and say finally, this is how it was.

A woman's reluctance to explore her past is entirely understandable, for to do so will insure neither her happiness nor her peace of mind. Whatever benefits accrue, will be small and quiet. At best, she can learn the theory: that what happened was not her fault. That she is not alone.

Just that. Just the facts. Just the fact that it's not her fault and that there's a lot of it going around. Just those facts, and these, so she can consume the theory and pass it on. At best, she can work towards prevention. At best, she can protect her children and exonerate her mother. At best, she can love other women. At best, she can love herself.

Toni A.H. McNaron

I
The Dream

"I'll cut my hair and have it tipped
I'm growing old
I fear that Aphrodite moans for me . . ."

So speak you sadly in my dream
in which you also say
        "I think I want to marry you."

It would be Aphrodite,
trainer of willowy girls,
imprisoning you on distant rocks
which only she can safely reach.
Alluring men, by looking soft,
you turn crystal sharp on touch.
Your musky goddess hates men,
sends them stony lovers who hold them
in contempt.

Did you know that
as you poured yourself into crêpe de chine?
I scan old photographs of you,
model posed in black:
were you in mourning?
"Zelda's double"—so your story always went.
You looked the same,
two Alabama belles;
you'd go to dances dressed in matching costume,
a plot to fool Fitzgerald,

172

on weekend pass from bootcamp in Biloxi.
Disguised, you waltzed divinely,
feeling the power of your masks;
next morning over tea and toast rounds,
you and Zelda tittered at your little joke
on handsome, clever Scott,
without regard for demons in his eye.

I look beyond the tintype pose
to see you caged in stays and buckles,
protected from the very ones you were to tempt.
That was her trick, great Aphrodite's trick,
because she really wanted you for her own,
but wouldn't say that,
wouldn't risk.

Now she moans to see you slipping from her grasp.
Unlike your first-born daughter,
I bring no swains to take your lure;
you're growing rusty, mother, not just old.
Your selfish mistress fears you'll soften,
wrinkle, grey,
and leave her.

In my dream, I hear you, unsurprised;
I sit and tell you tales of countless daughters
acting out our mothers' secrets.

II
The Myth

You bore me late, called me miracle:
said I cheered you up; saved you from depression;
brought you healing balm.
I was to be your private myrrh.

Choking
I stumbled through my childhood:
broke things, refused to eat;
had endless colds, sore throat, the flu.

At seventeen, I went fifty miles away to school.
I paid your price:
       wrote you what you wanted every day
       made weekly calls collect
       drove home on weekends to drink vodka you took
         for water.
Feeling the power of masks myself,
I hid my dreams
for fear you'd disapprove.

You died a decade later.
I stole a week from John Donne's sermons
and flew south to what I loathed and feared.
Your perfume lingered through the house
where your heart gave up.
I smelled you in every room,
choked, this time on bottled sweetness,
covering up your soured rage.

My sister sealed your coffin from all viewers.
No chance to see you dead.
That might have shed some truth
or brought me ease.

Through twenty-seven years, we never met or talked,
just hurled our hate and love across rooms
in which we sat politely, passions capped.
Now you rise unbidden in my dream:
dead these fifteen years,
you finally figure in my story.

III
The Song

Damaged and repairing,
I seize the skein of history from The Fathers.
We're in their picture, all us women;
the scene—a sacrifice at which we lie
on matching altars to a faceless god.
Each woman holds an icon on her breast:
mine looks like you;
yours is of your mother.
Our eyes are vacant sockets,
our mouths sewn delicately across,
elaborate stitches meant to silence us.

I vow to cut those fatal threads
that hold us in their myth
of Daughter-Saving-Mother;
to free our lips before it is too late.

To do this deed of daring,
I
pour my whiskey down the sink,
        begin to drink real water
go home to Lesbos where I find my goddess,
        Artemis, who clasps me to her, joyful
keep weekly vigil at my sacred fires,
        burning off sedge and thistle
        leaving space for me to grow
look across and find my long-lost lover,
        she no child and I no mother:
        asking for what we think we need,
        we don't attack each time we get it.
Last of all,
I
name the taboo web for what it is:
        cut the sticky films of family

that have kept me bound and gagging;
slash my mother out of me,
hear my father speak through me his hate of women,
fight my sister until we stand apart at last.

These labors done, I weep and wait,
open.
Then I sleep and dream this healing dream
from which I rise to weave us new.

So cut your hair, dear mother, have it tipped
and sing for Aphrodite if you must.
I see you walking on a beach beneath the waning moon:
I see me walk beside you, not at war;
I take our tangled strands,
lay them gently side by side,
and write this plain song whose forbidden key
eases the pain, replaces the noise
that kept us from each other.

REMEMBER

Yarrow Morgan

I

"Holy Mary, Mother of God,
pray for us now
and at the moment of our death."

My name is woman;
I live in an impregnable cage,
its limits set
by the vulnerable bruised edges of my body.
See this purple thigh?
See my crimson smile?
I sing as any creature sings
in a forest fire,
the high notes rise more intense
because the fire is invisible;
it's hidden cleverly,
tucked away in stray corners of my brain-cells.
Timers, set ticking before memory,
cause tiny flames of pain
to begin to lick me.
My name is woman;
I am so used to pain
I find myself uncomfortable
in any other element.

II

"Be quiet. Go to sleep now.
Mommy and Daddy are here."

Three-year-old girl child
lay in her bed,
drowsy and safe
awake not asleep.
She saw a pink and purple
wormlike thing above her body.
It did not touch her, no;
it pulsed in the air.
It was going to touch her.
Her screaming woke the house.
Woke her mommy who listened
and said, "It's not real,
it's not real; go back to sleep,
it's not real; it didn't happen."

III

"You were such a good baby, so quiet,
you could just sit still for hours!
You never cried."

She lay in her crib,
infant eyes open, unfocused—
only things very close were really seen.
Like the crib bars,
long and square and golden.
Her breathing sucks in and out
like curling ocean waves,
rolling up in swirls of pleasure
from belly to lips and back down again.
The space about her body seems infinite,
full of huge beings, strange smells;
and feelings vibrate as the dust-motes
in the air, that catch her eyes
and turn golden.
A being she knows comes close.

He touches her
and she is enveloped in safety.
He takes off her clothes
and she kicks her feet in the air laughing.
He laughs and tickles her.
Then he places upon her
the long, purple-pink globe of flesh
that has a life of its own.
It covers her body
from chest down to between her legs,
which are now forced back
and up into the air.
Her flesh curls inside her—
away from both him and herself.
She does not cry out.
She does not let herself know
any of the feelings
the vast air now swirls with.

IV

Blank it out.
Don't let yourself know it's real.
If it's real, you're crazy; blank it out.
Knowledge is powerlessness.
Blank it out.
Knowledge is pain.
Blank it out.
Mother to daughter;
blank it out.
Teach us to numb ourselves,
teach us not to feel.

The memory does not come easy;
it comes with screams that will not stop,

it comes with tears and terror,
with shame that I felt this,
shame that I feel this.
The memory does not come easy;
I tell you because I know,
I tell you because I will not be silent,
I tell you because I will not be silenced.

CONTRIBUTORS' NOTES

Jane Barnes: is a lesbian poet and fiction writer, who was for six years an editor of *Dark Horse*. She will bring out a book of poems called *Extremes* with her own press, BLUE GIANT PRESS, in June, 1981.

Paula Bennett: teaches Renaissance Literature at Northeastern and edits *Focus: A Journal for Lesbians*.

Susan Chute: is a lesbian/feminist writer who is an Associate Editor of the literary magazine *13th Moon*. She just started a women's writing workshop in New York City.

Sallou Cole: lives in San Francisco, California.

Kate Darkstar: lives in Minneapolis, Minnesota, and is recovering from chemical dependency, choosing to discontinue relations with her family members. She is presently working in non-traditional positions.

Naomi Falcone: is a lesbian separatist living in Northampton, working mostly with lesbians; part of an incest support group which did a T.V. program.

Noreen Firtel: is a hard-working poet, musician and part-time alchemist.

Gudrun Fonfa: is a lesbian feminist activist and freelance writer living in Woodstock with her daughter, Raven. She has published poetry, short stories, radio plays and newspaper articles, is interested in raising consciousness about fat women's oppression. "Daddy's Girl" won 2nd Prize in Washington Market Review Short Story Contest.

Teri Fontaine: is a former member of the Mermaid Poetry Collective (Boston), and is now editor and publisher for *a poetry mag*. She has two book-length manuscripts of poems, yet to be published. Her first published poem appeared in The Palm Beach (Florida) *Post* at age 12.

Christina Glendeening: is 34 years old and currently lives in the Twin Cities. She is a member of Iris Video Collective and has spent the past year completing "The Fear That Binds Us: violence against women."

Ran Hall: is a 36 year old lesbian feminist writer struggling with separatism and survival. She is an active participant in Womanwrites (Southeastern Lesbian Feminist Writers' Conference). "We can touch each other with words if we speak the truth."

Lark d'Helen: is attending Union Theological Seminary of New York City. She is forming a collective to produce media and teaching materials for church and social service agencies with a focus on physical and sexual assault issues handled from a feminist perspective.

Kathryn Ann Jones: is an artist, a teacher, a writer, a poet, a mother, a lesbian, a woman. She is currently working on several articles, poems, etc., including an article on lesbian custody cases.

Marti Keller: has been published in a number of small press anthologies, including one on erotic poetry, on the farmworkers, and on women and madness.

Joanne Kerr: is a Ph.D., a lesbian feminist writer, educator, and sociologist of art who is intent on changing individual and social consciousness through the reclamation, creation and nurturance of women's art, culture, myth, and ritual.

Anna Kore: lives in south Minneapolis, is a student at the University of Minnesota, concentrating in Women's Studies, child studies and writing. She supports herself and her son by working as a janitor. She has recently become involved in organizing a self-help group CAVEAT, Child Abuse Victims— Empathy and Togetherness

Anne Lee: wrote "Untitled Incest Piece" in 1980, when she was 33. Some of her identifiers were: lesbian, writer, mother, incest victim, fat, antipatriarchal, white, witch, friend. She lived in Pasadena, California, where she worked at Haven House, a battered women's shelter. In 1981 she helped found *Common Lives/Lesbian Lives* and moved to Iowa City, Iowa. Anne died of cancer in July of that year.

Donna Levreault: wrote this poem based on a dream where her male lover transformed alternately into her father and her brother.

Audre Lorde: is a Black, lesbian writer whose poems, essays and autobiographical writings offer a challenge to lesbians and non-lesbians, white and black, to examine their modes of handling differences in race, class and sexual preference.

Janice Maiman: was born and raised in the grand and terrible illusion of Coney Island. She has studied poetry with Joan Larkin, Jan Clausen, Carolyn Forche, Gregory Orr, and Ai. She has poems published in *Sinister Wisdom* and a short story in *Women: A Journal of Liberation.* At present, she is employed writing bureaucratic nonsense.

Dorothy McCracken: is a 36 year old, married woman who has been a Child Welfare caseworker. For the next few years, she hopes to combine motherhood with her life-long interest in creative writing.

Miriam: has lived the past few years in the foothills of the Cumberland Mountains in Kentucky, burning wood and hauling water, keeping bees and chickens, learning local flora, planting food. She has had copied 2 books of poetry: *Cynical Perfections,* about the city and *in silence that is full,* about nature and love.

Toni McNaron: at 44, struggles to articulate the connections between being a transplanted Southerner, a Lesbian, a writer of increasing voice, a teacher of mostly women writers at a large university in Minneapolis, Minnesota.

Karen Marie Christa Minns: is a New England poet currently living in L.A. Her work has appeared in *Sinister Wisdom, Black Orpheus, The DeKalb Literary Arts Review, Hudson River Anthology,* among others. A recent work, *Marking This Time: The L.A. Poems,* will come out soon from McBooks Press, Ithaca.

Yarrow Morgan: is a lesbian poet, a collector of lesbian history, and a Reiki healer who lives in Minneapolis, Minnesota.

Tracy Nagurski: is a 24 year old lesbian who has been writing poetry for ten years. She is working on a degree in Family Therapy and Chemical Dependency at the University of Minnesota.

Susan Marie Norris (Cygnet): after spending thirteen years as a teacher of English and as a school social worker, she found herself out of a job in 1971. Since then she has named herself as a lesbian, as chemically dependent, as an incest victim, as a musician, and as a poet. For the next two years, she intends to study feminist healing, and then join with a few women in a new healing center in Minneapolis.

Hia Perl: is a native Bostonian with a successful career as a mother and housewife.

Lee Ann Schlaf: lives in San Francisco close to the ocean. She runs in the park, plays the guitar and works as a counselor.

Snake: is a 34 year old Navy brat whose travels have included such diverse experiences as a motorcycle trip to Alaska, climbing in the Himalayas, and sailing in the South Pacific. She considers herself an adventurer, and lately has begun to explore the Himalayas of her psyche with Goddess worship, meditation and co-counseling.

Eliza Roaring Springs: lives in Berkeley, California with her dog Woody. She is a part-time gardener, masseuse, and proud member of The WholeWorks—a feminist theater collective.

Luisah Teish: is a Third World Feminist writer of Black and Native American descent; a member of Women Against Violence in Pornography and Media, Women Writers' Union, and Third World Women's Alliance. She writes poetry, drama, short fiction, and is a regular contributor to *Plexus, a Bay Area Women's Newspaper.*

T.: is an activist Lesbian-Separatist working on the *Lesbian Inciter/Insighter/Insider* newspaper. She trains in karate and intends to teach womyn to defend themselves and fight. She lives with two cats and enjoys her friends and running with the wind in Minneapolis.

Robyn Wiegman: is currently a Master of Fine Arts student in poetry at Indiana University-Bloomington where she works as poetry editor for the *Indiana Review.* She lives with her two cats, Emily and Freeway, and is working on a series of poems about beasts and mythical creatures called Imaginary Beings.

Terry Wolverton: is a lesbian writer and theater artist living in Los Angeles. She combines this work with community education and organizing; recent projects include the Lesbian Art Project, the Great American Lesbian Art Show, and the Incest Awareness Project.

Susan Wood-Thompson: is a lesbian feminist poet living in Washington, D.C. Her book of poems, *Crazy Quilt,* is distributed by Crossing Press.

Donna Young: in thirty-five years she's grown from Victim to Survivor to real person. In the process, she developed skills as a teacher, poet, mother and novelist, and is currently writing a sequel to her first novel, *Retreat: As It Was* (Naiad Press, 1979).

CLEIS PRESS

Cleis Press is a seven-year-old women's publishing
company committed to publishing progressive
books by women.

If you wish to order from Cleis Press please contact the office nearest
you: Cleis East, PO Box 8933, Pittsburgh PA 15221 or Cleis West, PO
Box 14684, San Francisco CA 94114. Individual orders must be pre-
paid and include 15% shipping. PA and CA residents add sales tax.
MasterCard and Visa orders welcome — include account number, exp.
date, signature and (MasterCard only) 4-digit bank number.

Books from Cleis Press

Sex Work: Writings by Women in the Sex Industry edited by Frederique Delacoste and Priscilla Alexander. ISBN: 0-939416-10-7 24.95 cloth; ISBN: 0-939416-11-5 10.95 paper.

Different Daughters: A Book by Mothers of Lesbians edited by Louise Rafkin. ISBN: 0-939416-12-3 21.95 cloth; ISBN: 0-939416-13-1 8.95 paper.

The Little School: Tales of Disappearance & Survival in Argentina by Alicia Partnoy. ISBN: 0-939416-08-5 15.95 cloth; ISBN: 0-939416-07-7 8.95 paper.

With the Power of Each Breath: A Disabled Women's Anthology edited by Susan Browne, Debra Connors & Nanci Stern. ISBN: 0- 939416-09-3 24.95 cloth; ISBN: 0-939416-06-9 9.95 paper.

Long Way Home: The Odyssey of a Lesbian Mother & Her Children by Jeanne Jullion. ISBN: 0-939416-05-0 8.95 paper.

The Absence of the Dead Is Their Way of Appearing by Mary Winfrey Trautmann. ISBN: 0-939416-04-2 8.95 paper.

Woman-Centered Pregnancy & Birth by the Federation of Feminist Women's Health Centers. ISBN: 0-939416-03-4 11.95 paper.

Voices in the Night: Women Speaking About Incest edited by Toni A.H. McNaron & Yarrow Morgan. ISBN: 0-939416-02-6 9.95 paper.

Fight Back! Feminist Resistance to Male Violence edited by Frederique Delacoste & Felice Newman. ISBN: 0-939416-01-8 13.95 paper.

On Women Artists: Poems 1975-1980 by Alexandra Grilikhes. ISBN: 0-939416-00-X 4.95 paper.